I CAN USE TOOLS

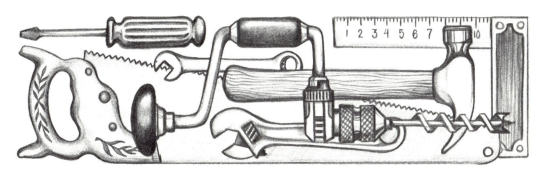

by Judi R. Kesselman and Franklynn Peterson

illustrated by Tomás Gonzales

ELSEVIER/NELSON BOOKS
New York

Library of Congress Catalog Card Number 80-26387   ISBN 0-525-66725-3
Published in the United States by Elsevier-Dutton Publishing Co., Inc.,
2 Park Avenue, New York, N.Y. 10016.
Printed in the U.S.A.   First edition
10 9 8 7 6 5 4 3 2 1

Tools help us make things. They also help us fix things. We use them to do jobs our hands can't do by themselves.

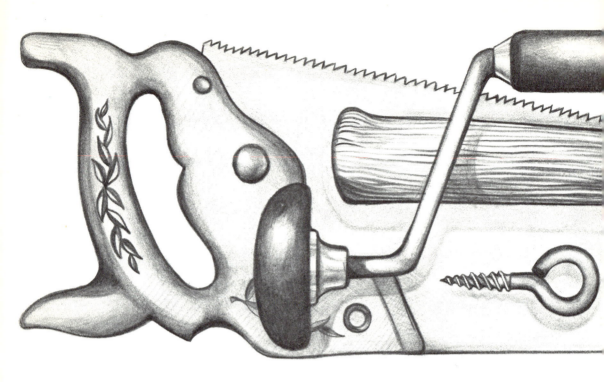

Each tool has its own special way of helping us.

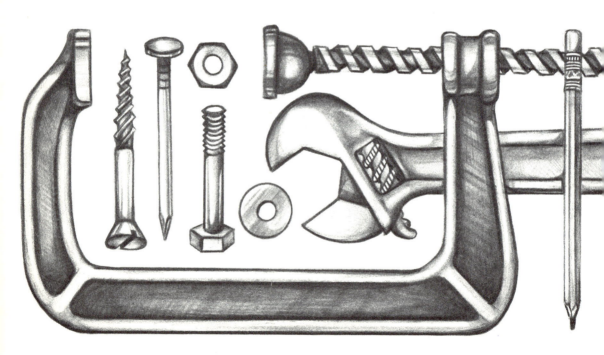

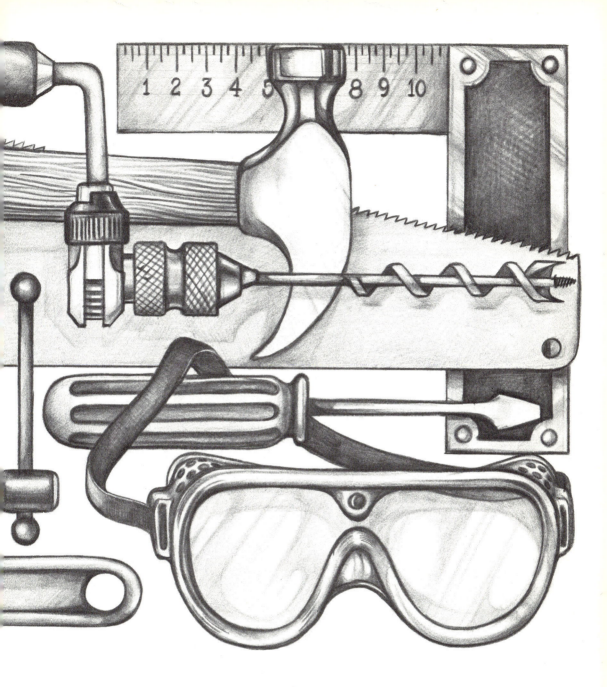

Once we know what a tool can do, we can use it to make hard jobs easy.

Carpenters use tools to build houses for people to live in. We can use the same kinds of tools to build small houses for birds. Let's see how that's done.

The first thing this builder does is to mark her board so she knows where to cut it. The **RULER** is a tool she uses to measure so that each piece of wood will be the right size for her birdhouse. Then she uses a

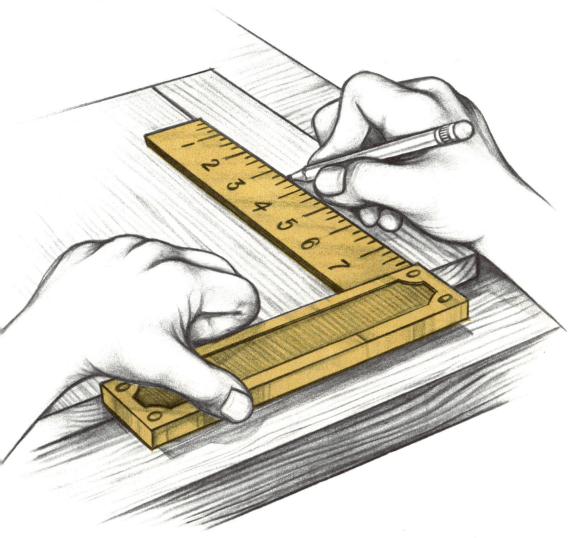

SQUARE and a **PENCIL** to draw straight lines on the board. These lines show her where to cut it. If the

builder measures and draws her lines carefully, all the pieces will fit together neatly. That's why a ruler, a square, and a pencil are such important tools.

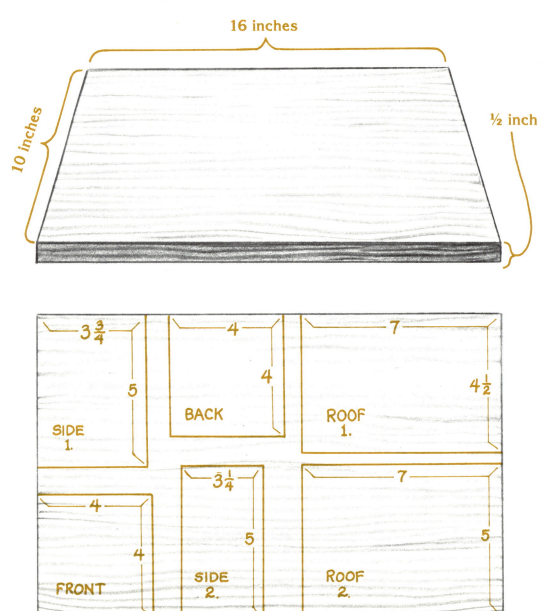

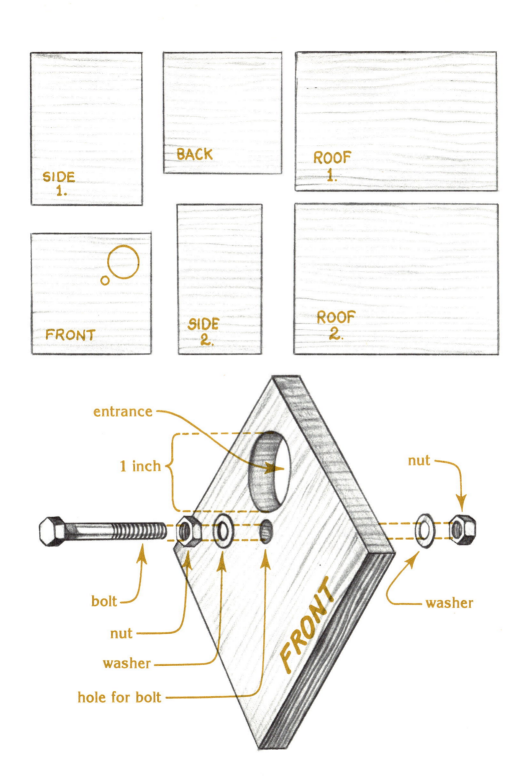

SIDE 1.

BACK

ROOF 1.

FRONT

SIDE 2.

ROOF 2.

entrance

1 inch

nut

bolt

nut

washer

hole for bolt

FRONT

washer

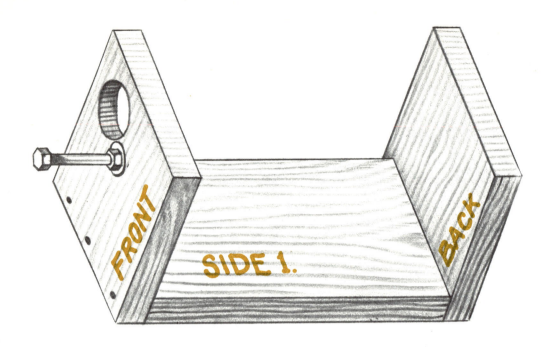

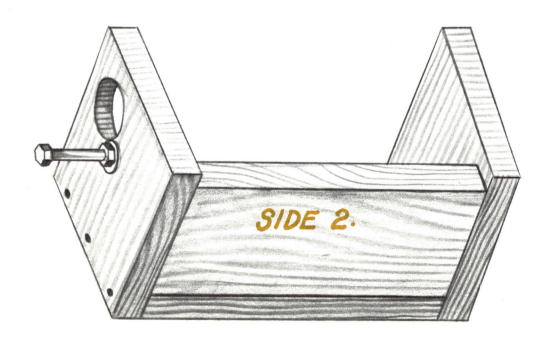

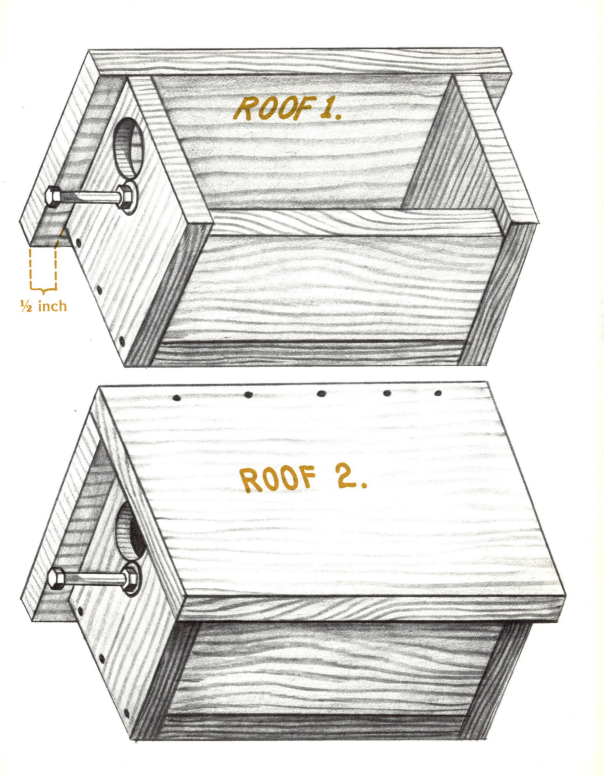

ROOF 1.

½ inch

ROOF 2.

After the boards have been measured and marked, they are cut with a **SAW**. This carpenter starts sawing by carefully putting the saw's *teeth* on the pencil line.

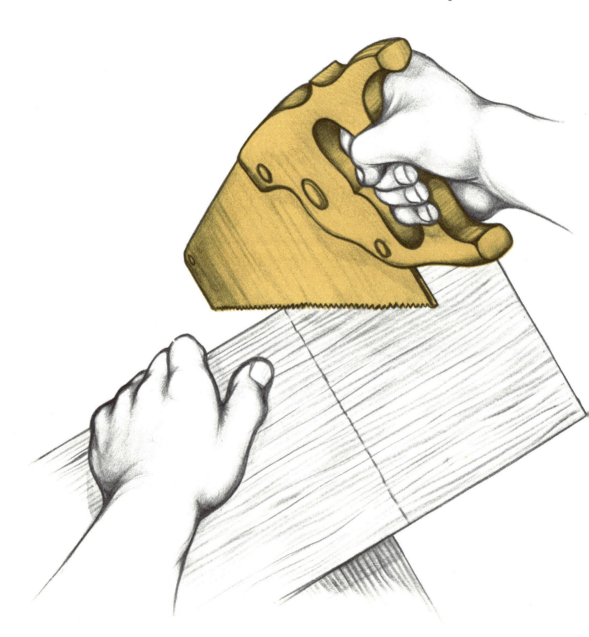

He moves the saw back and forth slowly until he has cut a little way into the board. Then he moves his arm in long, smooth strokes to slice the wood right along the pencil line.

If it is hard to hold onto a board while we saw, we get help from a **VISE**. It is fastened onto a work table. By turning the tool's handle, this girl can make the *jaws* of her vise grab the board tightly. Now she can saw it easily.

CLAMPS also help us hold boards, but unlike a vise, clamps can be moved from place to place. If we

wanted to glue the birdhouse together, we would use clamps to hold the pieces tightly in place until the glue dried.

This girl has decided to use **NAILS** instead of glue for her birdhouse. She uses a **HAMMER** to drive them into the wood. She begins by holding a nail in place between two fingers of one hand. With the hammer in her other hand, she taps the nail gently several times.

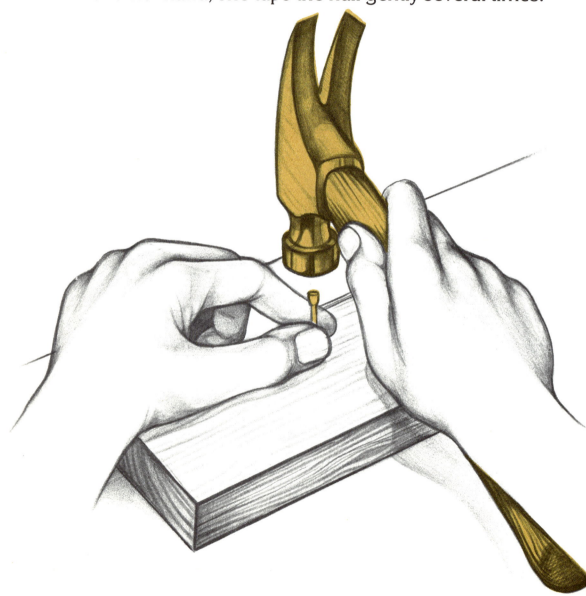

When the nail is hammered deeply enough to stand
up without being held, the girl takes her fingers away
so she can hit the nail harder.

Nails don't always go into wood perfectly straight. That's what happened here. This carpenter knows what to do. First he tries to straighten the nail by hitting it gently on its side. If that doesn't work, he'll

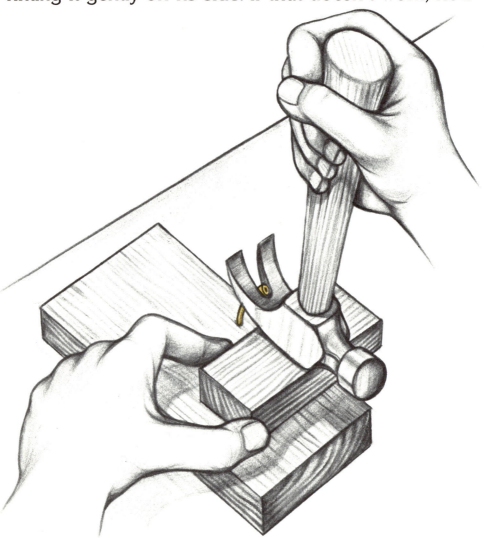

pull out the nail with the hammer's *claw* and start over with a straight new nail.

This boy wants to make his birdhouse very, very strong, so he is using a **SCREW** instead of a nail. He has put his **SCREWDRIVER** into the slot on the top of the screw. He turns the screwdriver to twist the screw

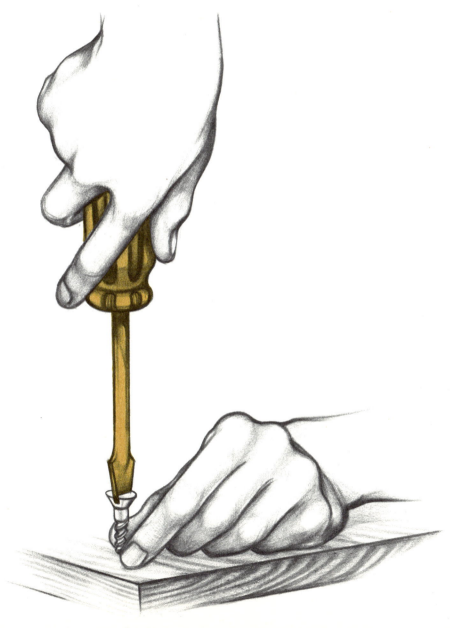

around and around. As the screw twists, it digs down through one piece of wood and into the other piece. The boy needs strong muscles to tighten the screw all the way. But when it is tight, it will hold his boards securely.

This girl is putting on a screw that will stick out part way. It isn't meant to hold her birdhouse together. It will be a perch for birds to stand on.

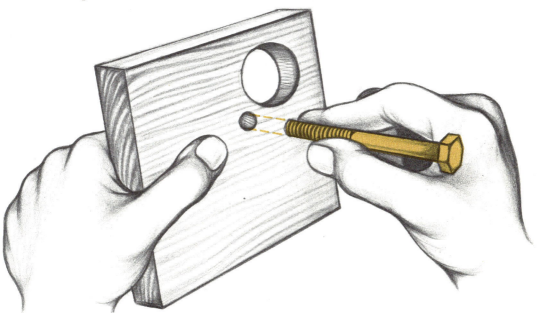

To make her birdhouse perch, this carpenter is using a **BOLT** instead of a screw. Bolts look very much

like screws. They both have spiral *threads* on them, but bolts don't come to points at the end. To tighten her bolt in place, the girl uses a **NUT**.

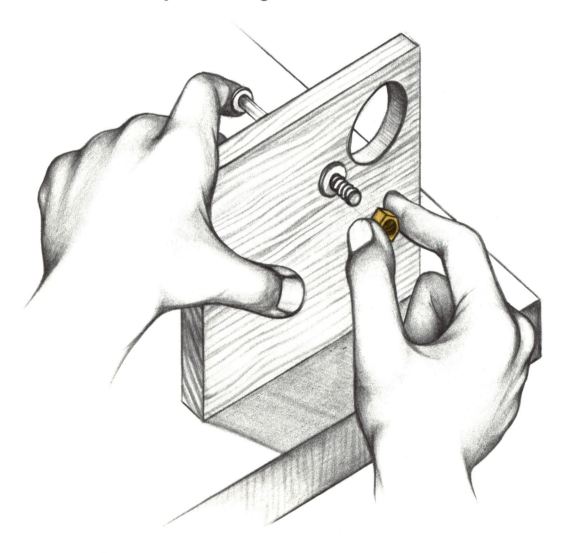

Her mother holds the nut in place with a **PLIERS**, while the girl tightens the bolt with her screwdriver.

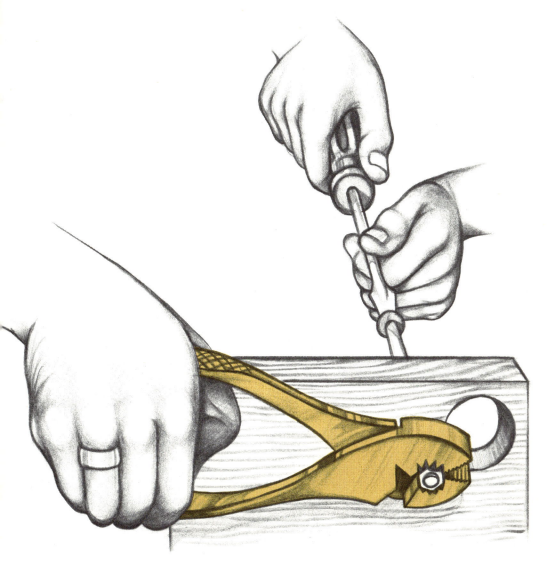

Pliers are like two metal fingers with handles. The tighter we squeeze the handles, the tighter the pliers squeeze the nut.

This boy is using the kind of bolt that can't be fastened with a screwdriver. He needs a **WRENCH** for

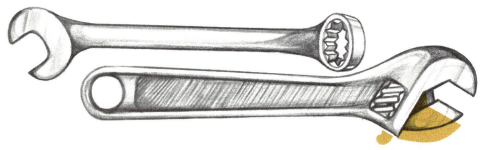

the job. Many wrenches fit only one size bolt or nut, but his *adjustable* wrench fits nuts and bolts of many different sizes. To fit a fatter bolt, the boy will twist the knob of the wrench so that its *jaws* open wider.

Nails, screws, and bolts come in many sizes and shapes. Some are made to handle very special jobs.

This *eyescrew* will soon help to hold the birdhouse high up in a tree.

Because bolts have flat ends instead of pointed ones like nails and screws, they can't make their own holes in wood. They need ready-made holes to fit into.

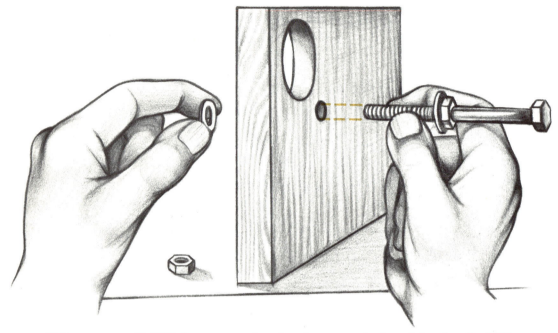

We use a **DRILL** to make holes and the kind of drill you see here is a **BRACE AND BIT**.

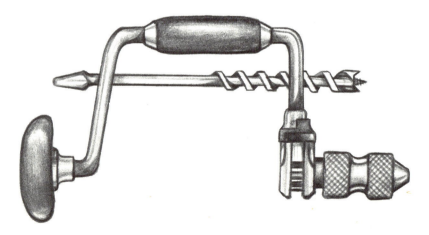

This boy is using a thin bolt for birds to perch on, so
he has put a thin bit into his brace. This girl has put a
fat bit into the brace. She will use it to make a big hole
that will be the door of her birdhouse.

The last step in building a birdhouse is to sand the wood until it has no splinters and feels smooth. For that we use **SANDPAPER**. Sandpaper comes in *coarse, medium,* or *fine* grades. It's easy to figure out which is which. Just rub your fingers gently across the three kinds, and you'll notice the difference.

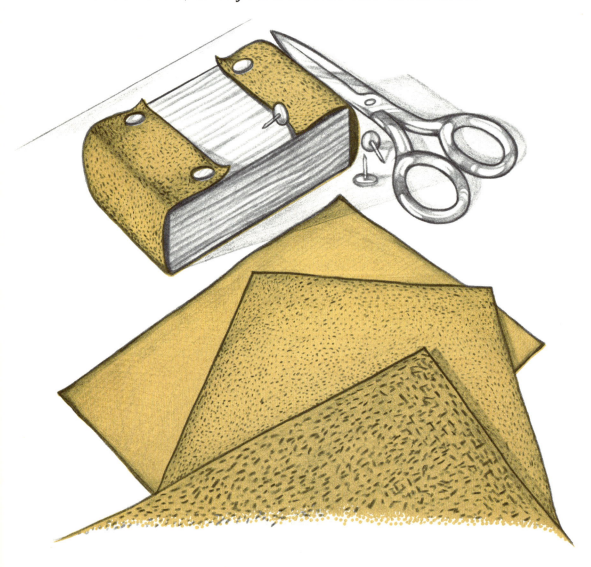

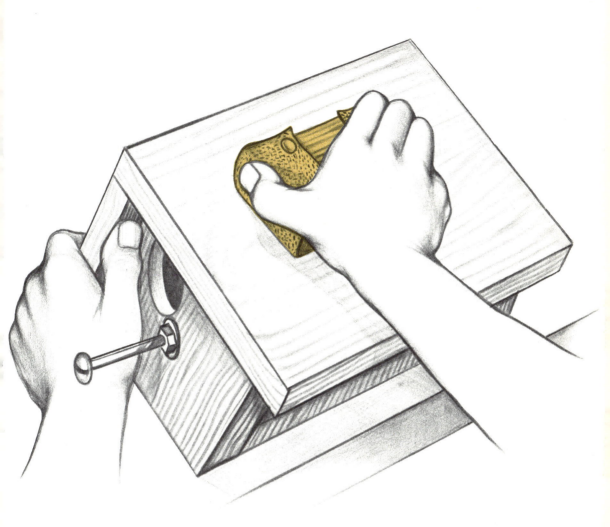

To finish her birdhouse, this girl first sands the parts of the wood that feel rough or splintery. She uses coarse sandpaper for that job. Then she rubs every surface of her birdhouse with medium or fine sandpaper until it all looks clean and feels smooth. To make sanding easy, she has wrapped the sandpaper around a small block of scrap wood.

This boy wants to paint his birdhouse. He has chosen a **PAINTBRUSH** that isn't too big or too small for the job. He knows that using exactly the right tool makes every job easier.

He knows, too, that if he wants his tools to last, he has to take care of them. After he uses it, he wipes each tool and puts it away in his **TOOL BOX.** That way, he knows that his tools will be ready whenever he wants to do the next job. And, most important of all— he will always be able to find them.

CONTENTS

'As a leader among academic leaders, Glyn Davis convincingly argues that more of the same is hardly the best survival strategy in a world of rampant technological change.

I spent eight years as a university chancellor but it was only when I read Glyn Davis's book that I finally understood the sector as a whole.

Just as monoculture puts ecosystems at risk, so too with universities. Diversity in the university sector will afford protection against impending technological disruption. Glyn Davis provides a compelling rationale for a progressive way forward.

Instead of convergence to sameness driven by ministerial control of fees, a liberated university system would encourage a rich variety of institutions from small to large, specialist to generalist.'

Alan Finkel, Australia's Chief Scientist

The Australian Idea of a University

Glyn Davis

MELBOURNE
UNIVERSITY
PRESS

MELBOURNE UNIVERSITY PRESS
An imprint of Melbourne University Publishing Limited
Level 1, 715 Swanston Street, Carlton, Victoria 3053, Australia
mup-contact@unimelb.edu.au
www.mup.com.au

First published 2017
Text © Glyn Davis, 2017
Design and typography © Melbourne University Publishing Limited, 2017

Cover design by Mary Callahan
Typeset by Megan Ellis
Printed in Australia by McPherson's Printing Group

National Library of Australia Cataloguing-in-Publication entry

A cataloguing-in-publication entry for this title is available from the National Library of Australia

9780522871746 (pbk)
9780522871753 (ebook)

PROLOGUE

When American sociologist William Lacy interviewed higher education and government leaders across Australia in 2015–16, he found much to like—a system that performed well in research and education, contributed to community, was admired internationally. Yet he saw challenges even in arcadia.

Over and over, Lacy reported the nation's university leaders lamenting the lack of diversity—a sense that Australia's public universities are much the same, all committed to research, comprehensive course offerings and large enrolments. This is an expensive way to deliver higher education, yet it offers few meaningful choices for students about the type of institution they attend.

According to one regional university vice-chancellor interviewed by Lacy, 'Australia has too many universities for its populations. It has too many campuses. It has too much duplication and too many trying to do the same thing. Something has to come and sort it out. It is either intervention by design or it is market forces'.[1]

Others perceive greater diversity among institutions— the harmonious landscape viewed from the bridge compared with the busy detail on the ground. 'I see a tapestry of difference,' remarks educationalist Sharon Bell. 'You see the cloak of similarity. The reality lies in the space in between.'[2]

This essay explores how shared origins, student expectations, academic culture and federal regulation contribute to a single idea of an Australian university. It celebrates the fairness of a model replicated across a continent, so students in Perth and Cairns enjoy access to similar institutions and course offerings. It notes that a single approach carries risk in an era of creative destruction. The public university developed in Australia over the past 170 years is vulnerable to disruption, whether by design or market forces. The future may benefit from greater diversity in higher education—less cloak and even more tapestry.

Any writing on universities joins a long conversation. There is much working from ideal types, abstractions of a university drawn from tradition and much-quoted authority. Somewhere still, Cardinal Newman writes in his study, calling on memory and imagination to propose an archetype for higher learning. Jill Ker Conway at Smith College seeks an education that addresses issues of central importance in women's lives, while Woodrow Wilson labours at all-male Princeton, determined to transform his young students into men unlike their fathers. The energetic Clark Kerr looks across the Berkeley campus and sees a multiversity, an institution expanding into ever-greater complexity.[3]

Their works sit alongside a vast library of books from former institutional leaders, each a bold or sly apology for their time in office, working from personal example towards some transcendent meaning of 'the university'. Such volumes sit alongside institutional histories, policy scholarship and fine defences of a broad and liberal education, as though enemies of such thought would linger long enough to read the argument. As academic and social critic Donald Horne reflected about honours supervision, 'Arguing over words: what could be more real?'[4]

All who write on universities face the gap between images and the lived experience—the campus filled with students and staff, who shuffle between unseen duties in strangely familiar buildings—the contrast between a specific place and expectations of an ideal. Not just *the* university but also *my* university, a weight of connections and memories, youth, friends and sensibility hard to capture. This concentration of experience resists reduction to neat definition. The English novelist Jill Paton Walsh evoked her Oxford not as a campus or town but a 'configuration of people, to whom one could never return this side of the lawns of paradise'.[5]

Each university is indeed its own world. Visit institutions across Australia and admire the differences. North Terrace in Adelaide offers a rich sample of academic buildings. Students and staff flow continuously between sandstone and contemporary edifices, some belonging to the University of Adelaide, others to the University of South Australia, each badged carefully to emphasise its institutional affiliation.

By contrast, the original Murdoch University campus sits alone in its own suburb east of Fremantle, with a bush court and buildings in the distinctive style of 1975. The University of Queensland fills its central quadrangle, the largest in Australia, with exotic trees and elegant lawns. When the jacarandas bloom in October, it is time to start studying for exams. Nature offers few such signals for students at the University of Technology Sydney—their classrooms are tightly fitted around the crowded city blocks of Broadway. The Casuarina home of Charles Darwin University has beach views, as does the Innovation Campus at Wollongong.

Academics live in the elegant suburbs or farms that dot the countryside near the University of New England, while prices in Sydney make housing an acute issue when hiring staff. Students walk under leafy trees amid beautiful stone at the University of Western Australia, and shoot hoops amid high-rise towers on a busy academic street at urban RMIT. There are campuses open late into the night, when weary part-time students fan out to distant car parks after class, others where teaching finishes at dusk. Some universities are located far from town, while others such as Macquarie benefit from a train station on campus, a large shopping centre and a hospital.

So many different campus designs, with scholars offering a countless variety of courses, amid institutional marketing that reveals the narcissism of small differences. The sheer scale of a sector with more than 1.4 million students and 120,000 staff means higher education is a realm of criss-crossing individual tracks, experiences and places.

Such apparent diversity can mask continuity of form. We live in detail but can think in generalities. The nation's public universities are not identical, and people value the special character of each institution. Yet they are all examples of a specific style of university, variants on a common model. Australia's public universities share assumptions about what defines a university—how it will be organised, what it will teach and research—an idea that stretches back into the past and points towards a common future.

The title 'university' implies shared characteristics—teaching to an advanced level, support for scholarship, classrooms and medieval gowns, a place outside the daily demands of life. Yet around the world diversity abounds. There are ancient comprehensive universities, technical universities, residential colleges. Universities with a disciplinary focus, those promoting a religion or characterised by scepticism. There are tiny institutions and huge campuses committed alike to engineering or agriculture. Universities for women in places where female education remains hard-won and under attack. Under a single label, the idea of a university finds many expressions.

Not so much, though, in Australia. This nation has avoided the monastic ambitions of Newman and the pieties of Wilson, and only occasionally rises to the uproarious ferment reported by Kerr. The nation has rarely hosted competing visions of tertiary education. Instead, from the mid-nineteenth century Australia embraced a single idea of the public university. Institutions would be owned by the state but be self-governing. They would be meritocratic and secular, at a time when many universities elsewhere claimed a religious or moral mandate. Australian universities would be comprehensive rather than specialist, teaching a wide range of professional courses. They would be commuter institutions, with only a small cohort living on campus. Most local students would travel from their parents' home or rent accommodation rather than reside in college.

This is a *metropolitan* model of a university, an institution of the city rather than a separate residential community. Metropolitan implies an urban setting, as opposed to a small and self-enclosed community set apart from the world. Like a city office block, a metropolitan university is a place people inhabit during the day, not a dwelling or a metaphysical ideal. It is a pragmatic and utilitarian understanding of the institution, fitting for a nation of practical people.[6]

The Australian university is metropolitan in a second sense. The Greek *mētropolis* means a parent city from which colonies arise. Here too the description is apt: from a single founding institution, the Australian idea of a university has spread nationally. Each new variant occupies its own geography and community, but draws from the parent in form and understanding of the enterprise.

The characteristic Australian university resembles its counterparts in London, Glasgow, Edinburgh and Dublin. In *What Are Universities for?*, Cambridge historian and essayist Stefan Collini observes:

> The British Empire led directly to the establishment of universities around the world modelled on the 'home' institutions, in practice more along the lines of London or the Scottish or larger civic universities than of Oxford and Cambridge.[7]

This was a resolutely British ideal—the influence of German research universities took decades to permeate, though eventually the British tradition accepted research as part of the university enterprise, building it into existing institutions rather than rethinking the model. There would be attempts to break away, radical new designs that started with promise but in time would come to resemble the standard national model.

Understanding why Australia chose this path for tertiary education is the subject of this essay. The aim is modest and specific: to explore how a nation scattered across an entire continent, in a world of competing models of higher education, settled on just one model.

It is to ask how history, values and policy interact to produce a singular Australian idea of the university.

The framing assumption is that diversity matters as a question of intellectual vitality and student choice—and as insurance. In a world of disruption, there are well-funded entrepreneurs around the planet keen to carve up higher education. The opening chapter traces the rise of for-profit competitors to traditional university provision. *Wired* shared the prediction of Sebastian Thrun, founder of Udacity, that 'in 50 years, there will be only 10 institutions in the world delivering higher education'.[8] Though universities have yet to experience the devastation endured by newspapers, the technology that can bring this about is already in place. How does an Australian public system offering just one basic model of the university cope in a world of unbounded study options?

Institutions are often 'path dependent', staying close to their original inspiration. The second chapter explores the founding moment—the reasons Australia has universities, and the way they are structured. Choices made in 1850 resonate still, as the metropolitan model developed in Sydney was copied around the colonies until Australia offered but a single category of university type.

Within seventy years of the establishment of the first Australian universities, prominent voices called for greater diversity. The third chapter explores numerous attempts to leave the track, including greenfield institutions built on the edges of cities, resolutely not metropolitan in character. These experiments left proud legacies, but they faltered as decisive breaks in Australian practice. They mark instead the limits of innovation in Australian public higher education. For however radical the starting point, in each generation bold experiments have been drawn, ever so slowly, back to the shared path.

Why has change proved so challenging? Chapter 4 argues that incentives to standardisation around the metropolitan model have proved strong—student preferences and academic culture both reinforce the customary pathway, and national policy has made it compulsory. In particular, decisions by a powerful minister more than a generation ago reinforced the singular Australian idea of a university.

Is this heritage also the future? The final chapter argues that path dependency continues only so long as key variables remain unchanged. As technological ferment threatens the established order, it also breaks the constraints that encourage conformity. It may be time to allow new choices, more diversity. The Australian idea of a university has served us well. It may also have run its course.

1

END OF THE LINE?

Universities, we learn, face imminent disruption. They may not endure amid a wireless world. Revolution looms while a teaching model with a millennium of history vanishes. There will be no more classrooms where lecturers can cast 'bogus pearls before real swine', as the Oxford political theorist and philosopher Isaiah Berlin once described undergraduate teaching.[1] Higher education, predicts the *Washington Post*, is 'headed for "creative destruction," a profound structural and economic shift in favour of employers, students and parents'.[2] *The Economist* offers a similar view: the three forces of rising costs, changing demand and disruptive technology will result in 'the reinvention of the university'.[3]

Creative destruction is a familiar trope. Digital media, delivered through the ubiquitous web, sweeps away newspapers, book publishers, video-rental stores.

The broiling inventiveness of entrepreneurs challenges, erodes, replaces. As one prominent technologist advises, 'demolition sets in motion the change necessary for innovation. A would-be innovator has to get rid of something in order to make room for something new to emerge'.[4] Silicon Valley becomes a symbol of such permanent undermining and reinvention.

Yet creative destruction is an idea with its own history. In the nineteenth century, philosopher Karl Marx spoke of capitalism destroying its own, undermining existing production with ever-more efficient techniques, driving down prices until the system collapsed. A century later, economist Joseph Schumpeter both expanded and modified the analysis. Capitalism, he agreed, is never stationary. It evolves constantly with improving technology and expanding markets. The old is overthrown from within as invention and competitors demolish existing local economies and create fresh industries. It is a cycle marked by frequent instability but not necessarily doomed to collapse.[5]

This was a good subject to ponder while on a train. To make his point, Schumpeter recounted the unintended changes to agriculture wrought by the Illinois Central Railway. Before the railway arrived, a local economy of small farms served the nearby Chicago market. They were close enough to transport produce to the city, yet protected by distance from competition. Prices were good and the local farms thrived—until the 1850s, when railways pushed into the Midwest. New tracks changed the economics of transporting produce, supported by advances such as grain elevators. The cost of freight fell to just a few cents a ton, quickly depressing demand for existing transport infrastructure such as turnpikes and canals.

The 'Main Line of Mid-America', as the train line to Chicago fashioned itself, changed the rules. Suddenly, large and efficient agricultural enterprises far from the city could freight in fruit and vegetables at minimum cost. The once thriving local agricultural economy collapsed, unable to compete on price or volume. Innovation instantly improved the lives of people in Chicago, through better and cheaper produce, but shattered nearby farming communities, which lost their livelihood. The Illinois Central Railroad delivered 'very good business' for some but a 'death sentence' for others, who fell victim to Schumpeter's 'perennial gale of creative destruction'.[6] The creativity of capitalism, led by entrepreneurs, constantly sweeps away the economy it calls into being.

Oxford experienced a similar shock. The university opposed an extension of the railway to the city, concerned that easy access to London might tempt 'improper marriages and other illegitimate connexions'. The argument was lost and a line opened in 1844. As in Chicago, there were winners and losers. Local coaching trade and canal traffic fell sharply. A long-established community of river fishermen could not compete with the 'large quantities of reasonably-priced, fresh and good-quality sea fish' freighted to the city by trains.[7] Internal migration in search of employment followed, along with manufacturing, and once-quiet Oxford grew rapidly.

Letters to *The Times* complained as 'the spirit of business and the clouds of smoke' pervaded the medieval city; the railway was changing forever the economy and character of Oxford. The sudden influx drew dark mutterings about the university becoming a cramming shop, where 'the railway brings in the fools and takes them away with their tickets punched for the world outside'.[8]

In 1844, as the railway reached Oxford, JMW Turner exhibited his masterful painting *Rain, Steam and Speed: The Great Western Railway* at the Royal Academy. Here was the Victorian vision of unstoppable progress. Through driving rain a train rushes across a bridge, powerful, irresistible and likely fatal to a hare that has strayed onto the tracks. New machines rip apart the settled world, a blur of steam and mist transporting the future. The novelist William Thackeray was impressed by the sense of animation in Turner's painting. 'Here comes a train down upon you,' he recorded.[9] Stand in the way, like some dissenting dons of Oxford, and the future may just run you over.

So I'm thinking about railways and the disruptive technology of the nineteenth century on a train to New Jersey. It is mid-winter, and New Brunswick is a long, cold ride from Penn Station in Manhattan. The New Jersey Transit leaves the city and suburbs until the scenery seems an endless process of small depressed towns strung along the line, many with closed factories lost to international competition. Few students alight from the clean but virtually empty train in January, leaving the streets of New Brunswick bleak and deserted. Yet for much of the year this is a lively place, one of several college towns hosting campuses of the State University of New Jersey. The coffee shops and pizza parlours lining the freezing walk from the New Brunswick train station to the front gates of Queen's College are closed for the New Year break. They serve a campus chartered in 1766 and later patriotically renamed for a hero of the American Revolution, Colonel Henry Rutgers.[10]

The university now bearing his name spans New Jersey and serves the 9 million residents of the state. Rutgers is the result of successive amalgamations, a combination of former independent colleges dotted around New Jersey. It operates from three regional centres. Like many Australian public universities, Rutgers must find ways to speak with staff and students scattered across many communities. It does so through extensive investment in teaching technologies, broadband connections that allow a Rutgers law professor in Camden to address a class in Newark, a study group in New Brunswick to include students across the network.

As usual, the promise is better than the delivery. Rutgers has excellent equipment, but watching distant figures on a plasma screen with slow refresh can be hard work. Still, the university sees itself at the forefront of a new delivery model for higher education. The campus remains the focus of the university experience for Rutgers students, while computers and television monitors link students to a richness of course material and teachers beyond the resources of any single site. In this, Rutgers again mirrors practice in many Australian public universities. The future becomes a blend of personal attention from the lecturer supported by online content and delivery. Such universities have embraced new teaching technologies, and should be safe from too much creative destruction.

Or so the Rutgers leadership thought until Phoenix appeared. Calling itself a university for working adults, the for-profit University of Phoenix offers a range of bachelor, masters and doctoral courses. Students can study online and attend local learning centres to interact with contract tutors. New classes start every five weeks, so there is no need for students to wait for an annual admission cycle. The offer is courses leading to employment—business but not arts, health administration but not social work. Students can work from home. Everything from attending classes to registration, even buying course materials, can be done through the internet.

In 1976, Phoenix was just one among many marginal US colleges, offering courses from a small campus but also by correspondence. It was not perceived as a threat by public institutions. Four decades later, Phoenix is America's largest accredited private university, claiming over 100 degree programs, nearly 1 million alumni and, at its peak, as many as 600,000 enrolled students. Phoenix boasts more students than any other tertiary institution in the United States and, likely, the world.

When I first visited New Brunswick more than a decade ago, Rutgers Vice President, Ray Caprio, recalled his first inkling of change. He had heard about Phoenix but was unconcerned. How could an internet provider, without research facilities or serious professors, compete against Rutgers with its history, scale and deep attachment to the people of New Jersey? Rutgers would always be the more desirable destination, with its attractive mix of campus life and interactive video teaching facilities.

Innovation always attracts sceptics. Many university graduates, Kaplan CEO Andrew Rosen insists, find suspect any tertiary experience unlike their own, 'and for a large percentage of the nation's elites, that means Gothic buildings, Frisbee on the quad, and Saturday football games'.[11] Yet if academics dismissed Phoenix, general staff at Rutgers seemed more impressed. Many wanted to upgrade qualifications for career advancement but could not face the high fees and lengthy courses of their own university. Several passed over Rutgers offerings to enrol in the Phoenix MBA program, attracted by its moderate prices and accelerated timetable. Intrigued, Caprio sponsored a staff member to undertake two courses at Phoenix and used the opportunity to assess the quality of course material offered by the virtual provider.

'Though all our academic prejudices make us want to discount Phoenix,' Caprio reported, 'actually the stuff was pretty good. Phoenix will stick to popular paying courses like the MBA and nursing. They'll never teach philosophy but they will be a force.'

Phoenix has achieved prominence in a landscape otherwise littered with e-learning failures. It has refined a business model that avoids investment in the expensive infrastructure of higher learning—those spires, cloisters, gargoyles and cumbersome overheads, such as tenured staff and libraries, that define a traditional university. Instead, Phoenix reaches out to students in America and beyond who want college education at reasonable cost and study without leaving home. Rutgers has spent vast sums on information technology to knit together three campuses in one small state, only to see a private competitor use the same equipment to span the entire American continent and, increasingly, the world. As Ray Caprio looked out his office window at desolate New Jersey in January, he could see a competitor not tied to a single place, bound neither by railway lines nor state boundaries. Here was the Main Line of Mid-America, a train rushing out of the mist.

Phoenix was no overnight success. It began with a curriculum delivered by mail and moved online in 1989.

Some reports suggest twenty-five years of cumulative losses before the university reached the scale necessary to make an online approach financially viable. Success brought serious challenges. Phoenix faced sustained criticism about marketing and enrolment policy. There were court battles, disputes over financial aid for students and internal disputes among shareholders. Enrolments fell and prospects dimmed, though the company was still valued at more than a billion dollars when traded in 2016.[12]

Where Phoenix pioneered, others followed. Private colleges founded by entrepreneurs, often with long histories in vocational education, saw an opportunity to challenge the public university sector. DeVry University began in 1931 as a training school, while Kaplan started the same decade as the Quest Education Corporation. Both became universities around the year 2000, tapping into growing demand for qualifications. With campus and online offerings, these have become large and sophisticated operations; Kaplan Chief Learning Officer, Bror Saxberg, is a recognised leader in learning sciences.

Though private higher education has been lucrative for a handful of providers it has proved a tough market for many, with numerous commercial failures. Promising online tertiary initiatives from prestigious universities, such as Columbia University in New York, produced embarrassing losses. A joint public–private venture in Britain labelled UKeU opened in 2001 and closed three years later with losses then valued at over £62 million. An MBA from Universitas 21 Global, an international network of research universities, faltered after modest enrolments. Making e-learning pay has proved difficult, but the survivors now lead the challenge to traditional universities. Online providers are the vanguard, and their revolution is streamed.

Ray Caprio grasped earlier than most the transformation heralded by Phoenix. Though e-learning still commands only a small portion of the market, here is a new business model for higher education, as online learning dispenses with a campus as the core of university life. The university becomes a virtual exchange connecting contracted teachers with paying customers. It is a business in which not academics but professional management makes decisions about hiring, course content and delivery in response to market signals. From the sunny American south arises a new creature, a for-profit approach to higher learning. For Rutgers in the frozen north, this is a worrying vision. Public universities have glimpsed the future, and it may pass them by.

CYCLES OF INNOVATION

The concept of an internet university runs sharply against the grain of tradition.[13] Universities are distinctive settings, not websites, tutorial chatrooms and Skype instructors. A sense of the university is shaped by history, familiarity and reruns of *Brideshead Revisited*. Phoenix is disturbing for some because it dispenses with every aspect of the standard package—a campus, lectures, laboratories, cafes and libraries, sporting clubs and student theatre. There is no rhetoric about building character or lifelong skills, no commitment to comprehensive knowledge (the 'universal' in 'university'). Education is about employment, an instrumental investment, and anything not essential to securing a qualification is jettisoned. In contrast to the solemn claims of public institutions, Phoenix does not assert that teaching and research are inextricably linked. On the contrary, this private institution shows no interest in original scholarship as an essential part of its university.

In the tradition of creative destruction, Phoenix proved to be only the first innovation cycle. It took numerous iterations before the mechanisation of cotton spinning and weaving achieved success,[14] so it is not surprising that higher education likewise provokes experimentation, with many attempts cast aside in the search for a viable business model. The innovator found itself challenged by new entrants. Phoenix maintained some familiar features of the public university—courses, academics and study centres if not campuses. With the rise of massive open online courses, a further insurgency questioned even the residual features of a university embedded in the Phoenix model.

This second cycle adopted the idea of a campus without walls but dispensed with the long-established outcome of higher education: the degree. In 2011, Sebastian Thrun and Peter Norvig from Stanford University offered the graduate-level course CS221: Introduction to Artificial Intelligence to anyone with an internet connection. More than 160,000 students signed on, two-thirds from outside the United States.[15] Enrolment did not count towards a Stanford qualification, but those who completed the course could receive a Statement of Accomplishment. Soon Silicon Valley shared stories of job seekers turning up with such statements rather than degrees, demonstrating proficiency in a particular software of interest to a specific employer. Why study for a four-year degree when employers need coders now and will hire on evidence of job-ready skills?

Massive open online courses—MOOCs—available for free online began with information technology subjects but blossomed quickly into other disciplines. Soon students could study any topic that interested an academic somewhere on the planet willing to produce content and support the vast numbers who might enrol. Harvard offered a MOOC on 'Hamlet's Ghost', the ANU one simply called 'Ignorance!' Students could peruse 'Bipedalism: The Science of Walking Upright' from Dartmouth or 'Sexing the Canvas: Art and Gender' at the University of Melbourne. Such topics attract 50,000 or more students on each offering, most of them graduates keen to keep learning. Universities that ventured tentatively just a few MOOC offerings have found themselves suddenly with a million or more additional students sampling their wares. Start-ups such as Coursera and EdX emerged to curate offerings, creating catalogues of courses. Coursera now reports more than 22 million registered users, including those keen to buy a credential that confirms their MOOC studies.

The MOOC success shows that technology could support tertiary teaching at scale. In January 2012, Sebastian Thrun left his teaching role at Stanford to found Udacity, a Silicon Valley education company with a mission to change the world. The popularity of MOOCs convinced Thrun that learning can be 'accessible, affordable, engaging and highly effective' and, importantly, offered at 'a fraction of the cost of traditional schools'.[16] Udacity planned to make computer science available online, then branch into related fields. It would replace lengthy college degrees with qualifications focused on getting people swiftly into information technology jobs.

Venture capital, excited at the prospect of new markets to conquer, rushed to support Udacity, which soon found premises in Menlo Park, California, and a young, talented staff. For visiting delegations, Sebastian Thrun shared his well-developed critique of existing universities and his vision for disruption. He contrasted the flexibility of Udacity with the governance issues plaguing older institutions. Thrun planned to avoid the bureaucracy endemic in universities; indeed, he promised to run his company without meetings or supervisors.[17]

The journey proved more challenging than expected, demonstrating Mark Twain's observation that education is 'the path from cocky ignorance to miserable uncertainty'.[18] Just as the first cycle of innovation saw many failures, so many second-cycle companies struggled. For Udacity, an ambitious partnership with San Jose State University came to grief, and the company pivoted towards vocational training. It launched 'nano degrees', short courses in areas such as data science, machine learning, web development and the Android operating system. The current Udacity program offers online instruction, coaching, career guidance and a ready-made portfolio for prospective employers. Udacity even guarantees relevant employment within six months of graduation or money back. Yet sometimes innovation is not enough; though the company reported enrolment growth, in April 2016 Thrun stood down as chief executive.

Other new entrants remain keen to succeed where Udacity struggled. Minerva is a San Francisco start-up that uses a standardised curriculum delivered on a proprietary online platform. When founder Ben Nelson is feeling expansive, he claims Minerva will replace the liberal arts college with courses that can be delivered around the world. Using a direct-instruction approach developed for school students, Minerva ends the independence of academics to design their courses. Instead, students access a highly structured curriculum that controls precisely the content conveyed. Regular online quizzes test student comprehension before moving to the next concept. Designed to challenge an Ivy League education, Minerva offers a college experience at half the price of traditional university tuition and accommodation. There are no lectures, so 'the professors can live anywhere, as long as they have an internet connection'.[19] This is not a university as a collegiate institution, with staff offices and libraries, but a consortium of teachers and learners linked by technology.

With an annual entry of only 220 students, it will take Minerva some time to spark radical change. Yet Minerva is only one of countless new institutions being founded. Change is in the air. Content has become 'free and ubiquitous', notes Daphne Koller, who helped found Coursera. The only universities that will survive, she contends, 'are the ones that reimagine themselves in this new world'.[20]

DISRUPTING THE PUBLIC UNIVERSITY

While private education makes inroads, millions of students continue to enrol in traditional higher education offerings. Reports of the death of the public university are much exaggerated. For most students, higher education is about knowledge rather than just content, and here context and immersion matter. Still, no one misses the intent. Entrepreneurs plan to break the university monopoly on tertiary qualifications. Phoenix transferred existing academic offerings to an online world. Sebastian

Thrun went a step further, taking apart the traditional university offering. Degrees could be broken down into individual courses, and eventually into single competencies, each sold separately.

This 'unbundling' of universities resembles the trajectory of recorded music, from buying albums in a record store to downloading individual songs online. Ever shorter offerings make content more digestible—degrees can be 'broken into modules; modules into courses; courses into short segments'. Lecturers are told, without much evidence, that six minutes is the ideal time for a video explaining a new concept, and four weeks the course duration most likely to hold student attention through to completion.[21]

For students, the arrival of online educators provides an alternative to the campus-based public university with its familiar menu of degrees, semesters and academics concerned with garnering time for research. Phoenix offers a frankly utilitarian narrative: university is not a place for leisurely self-exploration or the slow accumulation of graduate attributes. It is about securing a better-paid job with the lowest student debt possible. Since a qualification is essential in much of the labour market, universities stand between people and employment.

Some entrepreneurs now question the worth of any university credential. Why study at all? Business magazines publish lists of billionaires who never attended, or quickly dropped out of, college—notably Bill Gates and Mark Zuckerberg.[22] One co-founder of PayPal, though himself a graduate of Stanford Law School, argues that tertiary study is just following old career tracks. Winning a place at a university should suffice; for the truly talented there is no need to spend years on campus. The

Thiel Fellowships—$US 100,000 over two years—reward young people who put aside study to focus instead on a new business idea.

Critics of this attack on tertiary education note that people will have richer, healthier lives if they finish their degree. Research shows the best-performing new ventures are not invented by 20-year-old college drop-outs but 'started by alumni with about 10 years of professional experience after graduation'.[23] Still, thousands apply for a Thiel Fellowship each year, hoping to be rewarded for not going to university.

Not every entrepreneur seeks to disrupt the entire university experience. Some in the edutech sector hope to colonise specific steps in the teaching cycle—the design and delivery of course content, student learning, detecting plagiarism and contract assignment writing, recruitment and admissions processes, online tutoring services, third-party fund-raising and alumni relations. They offer simulations to aid learning, new student credentialing processes, promises to match graduates with jobs. This new private market raises the prospect of a 'plug and play' university, an online institution that contracts out every aspect of its operation, from teaching to administration. The stakes are significant—some $40 billion in venture capital supports projects to take over aspects of the familiar public university.[24]

———

For the Illinois fruit farmers and Oxford river fishers, creative destruction came quickly. New technology arrived on rails, and ended abruptly an older way of life. Many predict universities face the same swift falls in audience and revenue experienced by newspapers and free-to-air television. *The Economist* laments the 'many towns and cities' about to lose valuable income as universities decline.[25] Yet despite the predictions, public higher learning continues to grow.

Schumpeter may not be surprised. He observed that creative destruction is not necessarily incessant; revolutions can 'occur in discrete rushes which are separated from each other by spans of comparative quiet', much as punctuated equilibrium may mark the process of evolution.[26] Public universities have moved swiftly during pauses to anticipate and respond to market changes. They spawn their own online degrees, adopt nano qualifications and mirror private providers in offering students 'badges' that attest to skills acquired beyond the classroom.

Staff from public universities crowd conferences on the coming change, adopting the language of those dedicated to destruction. Once only entrepreneurs talked of 'stackable qualifications', enabling aggregate degrees drawn from the programs of many providers. Now Silicon Valley finds unexpected competition from the public sector. Institutions such as Arizona State University rework curricula for online delivery and form alliances with Starbucks to roll out employee education programs. Georgia Tech in Atlanta has transferred its prestigious Masters of Computer Science to web delivery, offering an internet version of the degree for less than 20 per cent of the cost of studying on campus.

In Indiana, former Governor and now President of Purdue University, Mitch Daniels, surprised staff and legislature alike when his public university purchased private Kaplan University. By acquiring an additional 32,000 students, fifteen campuses and 3,000 employees operating without the constraints of public ownership, Kaplan U provides Purdue with a new channel to students across America. Some view the deal as 'as an exciting evolutionary step for public higher education', others as a 'dangerous threat'.[27] Few predicted public universities would start buying their private rivals.

The contest for students has also encouraged a return to basics. Faced with an online challenge, many public universities stress the full campus experience, much the way rock bands shift focus from recordings, which are easily obtained, to live performances, which remain a rare and personal experience, impossible to reproduce on the web. The peril of creative destruction has seen surprising new expenditure on impressive buildings and teaching facilities, in particular student accommodation, all designed to entice students back to campus. Recruitment processes stress the cohort experience, a like-minded group of enduring friends first encountered on campus.

Back at Kaplan, CEO Andrew Rosen believes a 'back to basics' campaign by public universities will not be sufficient to save familiar institutions. Twenty-five years from now, he predicts, tertiary education will be structured around mobility, allowing students to choose courses from multiple providers. Learning will be more personal, focused on individual outcomes, offered in ways that are more accessible, global and just 'cooler'. These trends, he concludes, are 'inevitable'.[28]

Entrepreneurs see public universities as still provider-driven, organised for the convenience of academics with long summer breaks as time for research. They suggest this is no longer acceptable to students with many new choices. This alternative vision of higher education challenges the unique role of the university in generating and sharing knowledge. It calls into question the idea of a degree, the necessity for a special place called 'a university'. The first innovation cycle made study accessible to those who might otherwise miss out on tertiary education. The second reminded the world that a standard tertiary qualification is not the only valuable certification. A third cycle—and those sure to follow— will nibble away at the tertiary sector until, perhaps, the familiar model of a public university falls beneath the wheels of creative destruction.

To endure, the public university will need resilience and innovation. Its friends should also encourage experimentation. There are numerous alternative models of higher education worth trying in Australia. With more variety, more institutions can find ways to thrive. Even in a world where information is pervasive, judgement and expertise will still be honed through encounters with scholarship.

For Australia, this is a challenge with particular urgency. The nation has developed an idea of the university that makes university study accessible and consistent across Australia. Yet it is a model with a singular lack of diversity. Australian public universities are alike in key ways—they are large, highly regulated, largely non-residential institutions offering standard degrees, linking research with teaching, stressing familiar pathways to professional standing. If new modes of study attract large numbers of students away from existing public universities, the sector will prove vulnerable to changes emanating from Silicon Valley and entrepreneurs closer to home.

From his campus by the rail tracks in New Jersey, Ray Caprio has seen the rise of Phoenix as evidence the future of public universities cannot be taken for granted. Other venerable institutions have vanished, and a thousand-year tradition is no guarantee of continued viability. Creative destruction, like Turner's train, hurtles towards us all.

2

THE METROPOLITAN UNIVERSITY

We choose a path and thereafter it leads us—the 'deep lane insists on the direction', as TS Eliot wrote in *East Coker*. The further we go, the more we commit to this course; other choices fall behind, those paths not taken. Over time, this seems the only road possible. For universities in Australia, the path chosen early still guides the bearing. An Australian idea of a university, developed in colonial society but keenly influenced by British heritage, has shaped all local universities since 1850.[1]

The pattern set by those original choices produced the metropolitan university, with core characteristics and numerous overtones acquired through a shared history. Over time the institutional model chosen first in Sydney, and shortly after in Melbourne, became the standard Australian university. It served as an ideal type, infinitely transportable, able to be recreated in new settings. The model extended from city to city, modified with experience and expanded as new professions emerged, but essentially developed along the original path. When legislators sought to break the mould and create very different universities, they found the original model hard to resist.

An ideal type can shape public policy until familiarity renders invisible the assumptions that informed the very contours of the type. Once established and shared, a model of what constitutes a public institution will make any alternative seem inadequate—not a 'real' university. The ideal type directs choices, encouraging us to create the same institution over and over, despite attempts to innovate. The Australian idea of a university has served the nation well—all the more reason it endures—but delivers a narrow range of institutions, a singular understanding of the university.

This underlying continuity can be disguised by surface changes. Universities are contemporary institutions, apparently much altered over the past century and a half. Once a small community with a single cafeteria where everyone ate and conversed, employing familiar departmental secretaries for the provision of advice, and priding itself as a place of personalities and campus fame, the university has grown to unprecedented scale. During the early colonial period, only a handful of people could access tertiary study. By contrast, in contemporary society nearly 40 per cent of young Australians enrol at a university.

With 50,000 or more students, many universities now offer the amenities of a large town, with standard rules and procedures to deal with complexity. Growth has occurred despite declining public investment in each student. The sector is larger, less personal, more competitive. Scale has encouraged the use of management processes once the preserve of commerce. Universities have 'taken on more and more functions that require significant administrative capacity'.[2] In turn, these developments encourage critiques of the corporate university.[3]

Still, enduring patterns remain. Form has not overwhelmed function. Behind the new facade an older set of decisions continues to influence higher education. The Australian public university remains city-based; it is a publicly owned but independent, meritocratic and commuter institution; the scope of its interests is comprehensive, with a strong inclination to professional education and a commitment to research. Its mode of instruction, and even the spread of enrolments across its disciplines, suggest considerable continuity. The Australian idea of a university, developed in the 1850s, has evolved—but much abides.

Hence the concern: if Australian public universities are more alike than different, then disruption from Silicon Valley may affect the whole sector, simultaneously. The Australian university system consists almost entirely of those institutions targeted by entrepreneurs for creative destruction, namely, large public institutions offering a standard product. What looks like difference close up loses distinctiveness from a distance. We locals might perceive important variation between the University of Southern Queensland and the University of Western Australia, but seen globally they look alike: both are campus-based, publicly funded institutions pursuing research and offering the same range of degrees, from bachelor to doctoral qualifications in a broadly similar array of fields.

International classifications underscore this uniformity of Australian institutions. For nearly fifty years, the Carnegie Commission has classified every type of higher education institution operating in the United States, a nation that hosts a wide array of institutions. The result is the most rigorous typology available of higher education forms. The Carnegie 'basic classification' identifies seven types of higher education, with thirty-two varieties of institution. The schema does not yet include institutions such as Udacity, but makes clear that higher education in the United States encompasses many different organisational forms and an array of missions and scales.[4]

Transfer the seven basic Carnegie types to Australia, however, and every public university falls within a single category: the doctoral university, marked only by varying degrees of research intensity. So do private universities such as Bond and Notre Dame. There is only a single private liberal arts college in Australia, just one university of specialisation, and a handful of dual-sector institutions, offering both tertiary and vocational courses, a type not recorded by Carnegie.[5] Classified by mode of education and highest degree offered, Australian universities are remarkably similar—described by one journalist as 'unique, in the same way'.[6]

PATH DEPENDENCY

Why have Australian universities retained so many of their founding characteristics? An answer is suggested by the concept of path dependency, a theory developed in economic and historical analysis and now applied to many aspects of institutional life. The creation of new universities is a rare and expensive act. The first institutions were informed by the needs of the colonies and prevailing thinking about the role of the university. This original model, now well established and perceived as successful, travelled across the nation.

Path dependency explores the lasting influence of founding ideas, the ways in which an initial choice shapes subsequent options.[7] Models of path dependency focus on a 'critical juncture' that has a lasting power over institutions, reinforcing patterns of behaviour and understanding of purpose.[8] Once the key features of an institution are established, the organisation has committed to a particular model. It becomes costly to contemplate major change in direction, and may be challenging conceptually because the original form and mission of the organisation seem comfortable and apparently logical.

The power of a starting point to shape outcomes is often illustrated by the QWERTY keyboard.[9] The QWERTY keyboard was developed in the nineteenth century to overcome jamming in typewriters. The design separated commonly used letters so that the striking of proximate keys in close succession would not cause mechanical failure.[10] This requirement is now obsolete, yet QWERTY remains the standard, transposed from keyboards to computers and mobile phones. An early decision in keyboard design to address mechanical failure influences the technological path long after the initial reason fades.

Studies identify similar path dependency in other technologies, the development of institutions, the location of cities, origins of government policies and the formation of law and language. As political science professor Paul Pierson cautioned in a study of the welfare state, once we start down a pathway it becomes 'hard to reverse'. We adapt to the familiar, making commitments that 'render the costs of change (even to some potentially more efficient alternative) far higher than the costs of continuity'. Hence, 'existing commitments lock in policymakers'.[11]

There are limits to path dependency arguments, which might otherwise say little more than 'history matters'.[12] Not every starting point becomes a set pattern, just as not every current practice is simply the inevitable next step in an original set of decisions. Political scientist Herman Schwartz argues that if small 'contingent causes at the beginning of a path' are to encourage continued adherence there must be 'increasing returns' to political and social institutions.[13] The original reasons for the path must be compelling, and must continue to deliver benefits over time.

Path dependency is a way to think about historical causation, but to persuade as analysis it requires clarity about a starting point and the influences that keep an institution headed in a particular direction. As will become apparent in this essay, a series of original ideas for an Australian university made sense in context, and remain convincing. Choices from 1850 proved intelligent responses to local needs and understanding. As sensible decisions across time, they have endured. In time, those founding ideas have been reinforced by the preferences of Australian students for professional programs, by academic norms about the character of a university and by public policy that imposes homogeneity. Social scientist Scott Page suggests such path dependency is based on 'increasing returns, self-reinforcement, positive feedbacks, and lock-in'.[14] A practical institution is also an ideal, shaping the very definition of what it means to be a university in Australia.

At key moments during the twentieth century, policy makers questioned the value of a narrow model and pressed for more variety. We will explore the challenge of pushing against an established practice. Students and staff alike preferred the status of existing arrangements, and federal ministers found it convenient to impose a uniform regulatory regime for the sector, thus making difference difficult to sustain. Convention overwhelmed invention. New players were drawn back, slowly but firmly, to the existing settings. A single idea of a university has ensured that any new public university resembles those already operating.

A BRITISH SETTING

Along with parliaments and guns, the English language and rum, the concept of a university was imported with the first European settlers. This inheritance was expressly British in character, part of the nineteenth-century spread of higher education across the British world. As historian and political scientist Tamson Pietsch reminds us in *Empire of Scholars*, new institutions were set up by 'self-confident settler elites who saw them as both symbols and disseminators of European civilisation in the colonies'.[15] Universities were founded at Madras, Calcutta and Bombay in 1857 and in Otago in 1869. In Canada, the King's College began in 1827 as an Anglican institution of higher learning. After decades of internal wrangling, the college was renamed in 1850 as the secular University of Toronto.[16]

This British influence was decisive when Australian colonies came to debate tertiary education. Colonial authorities might have found inspiration in the research universities of Germany or the great private colleges of the United States, but instead focused only on British practice. As with other universities of the empire, any Australian variant would exhibit loyalty to home. Since there was not just one British idea of a university in circulation, however, Australian legislators would devise their own version of British tertiary education, a blend drawn from practice in England, Scotland and Ireland.

Britain in the middle of the nineteenth century was marked by social unrest following rapid industrialisation, the growth of cities, the rise of popular newspapers and agitation for the vote. Riots and recessions made governments sensitive to popular sentiment. This was the moment Charles Dickens published, instalment by instalment, his *Bleak House* with its vivid depiction of a dysfunctional legal system and grim private schools. Liberals pressed for restrictions on child labour, for better public sanitation, safer factories, free trade, religious tolerance and, sometimes, equality of rights for women.

Scepticism about the established order extended to universities. In England, ancient institutions dominated tertiary education, imposing religious tests for student entry and restricting offerings to a handful of degrees. Reformers sought to open higher study to a broader spectrum of society, and in 1826 established London University under the intellectual influence of reform-minded thinkers Jeremy Bentham and James Mill. London University offered higher education to those excluded from Oxbridge by faith or low income, including non-conformists, Catholics and Jews. The new institution taught in fields other than classics, mathematics and ancient languages, and offered education for the legal and medical professions. Some courses allowed women to enrol, a move that would be resisted for decades at older universities.

London University was firmly based in the city and did not require residence in college. It offered a broad curriculum in 'modern science, modern languages, the major branches of philosophy, and political economy'.[17] In addition, the university taught engineering, mechanics and chemistry. Only one popular branch of higher learning was excluded: there would be no classes in theology.

Soon enough London University spawned a competitor, set up by dignitaries such as the Duke of Wellington who opposed the idea of a 'godless university'. Established in 1829 as an Anglican institution, King's College London accepted the logic of a more inclusive curriculum and enrolment, but not the exclusion of religion. The rivalry did not last long; in 1836, London and Kings joined as the University of London to offer a wider variety of instruction, with a prominent role for professional education in a largely secular urban setting.

The example of the University of London would influence Australian practice, along with developments in Scotland and Ireland. In Edinburgh and Glasgow, the Scottish Enlightenment fostered a number of universities as non-residential and non-sectarian institutions, with provision of education on merit. Scottish universities differed from some English counterparts by offering large lectures rather than the individual tutorials of the kind provided by colleges at Oxford and Cambridge. This teaching approach would be mirrored in Australia, along with the Scottish innovation of an honours year— first adopted by the University of Adelaide, which introduced the option of a fourth year of study in 1901.[18]

In Ireland, three new institutions were founded from 1845 as Queen's College Belfast, Queen's College Cork and Queen's College Galway. All were established as secular institutions, to deal with religious divisions in Irish society and encourage a strong focus on the professions. They would be united in 1850 as Queen's University, one of many institutional experiments with higher education in Ireland.[19] Though Catholic and Protestant clerics alike condemned these 'godless colleges', the institutions drew enthusiastic young students from across Irish society.

For Irish Catholics, long excluded from Trinity College in Dublin, the new institutions provided opportunity and wider intellectual horizons. Not all Catholic intellectuals, though, welcomed the inclusion of professional programs or focus on employment outcomes. In 1852, John Henry Newman, the rector of the new Catholic University of Ireland, published his voluminous *The Idea of a University*. Newman rejected professional education and argued instead for knowledge as a worthwhile end in itself. He favoured a liberal education, delivered in an institution that was male, collegiate, literary, residential and focused on teaching.

More than a century later, Newman's aspiration to inform character through great teaching influenced the 1963 Robbins Report into British higher education:

> It is the essence of higher education that it introduces students to a world of intellectual responsibility and intellectual discovery in which they are to play their part ... The element of partnership between teacher and taught in a common pursuit of knowledge and understanding, present to some extent in all education, should become the dominant element as the pupil matures and as the intellectual level of work done rises.[20]

Though the concern for teaching resonated, the organisational form proposed by Newman was hostile to innovation in university education. He spoke against the spirit of his times, rejecting a curriculum informed by metropolitan values or teaching led by research. Instead, Newman offered an idealised Oxford of his youth, distant from the city, a place for quiet reflection. The vision failed in translation. The Catholic University of Ireland struggled to attract sufficient students or supporters and Newman resigned after three years as rector.[21]

As Australian legislators came to contemplate a local university, they could draw ideas from debate within Britain about how a university could 'provide a home for attempts to extend and deepen human understating in ways which are, simultaneously, disciplined and illimitable'.[22]

The spirit of the age questioned received wisdom, including long-established patterns of university education. A Royal Commission in 1850 delivered tough judgements about Oxford and Cambridge and insisted on major reform. Public intellectuals argued for contemporary and relevant universities. Herbert Spencer published *Education* in 1861, and FW Farrar his *Essays on a Liberal Education* in 1867, the year John Stuart Mill presented an inaugural address at St Andrew's University. There, Mill called for a modern education, one that liberated rather than indoctrinated young minds. It was time, he suggested, for ancient universities to stop pursuing 'the repression of independent thought, and the chaining up of the individual intellect and conscience'.[23] Here was reform in full song, a call for relevance and contemporary knowledge at just the moment colonial administrators in New South Wales turned minds to establishing a university.

ORIGINS OF AN AUSTRALIAN UNIVERSITY

There was no Australian nation in 1816, and no Australian universities. An aspiring student must sail to Britain, as did William Charles Wentworth, likely the first Australian to receive a university education. Wentworth studied law in London, travelled in Europe and spent time at Cambridge. He returned to Sydney in 1824 to make his reputation as a barrister, publisher and, in time, legislator.

From 1849, Wentworth led the argument in the New South Wales Legislative Council for an Australian university. He joined a circle of Sydney notables who believed the new colony needed trained professionals. A university in Sydney, said Wentworth, would 'enlighten the mind', 'refine the understanding' and 'elevate the soul of our fellow men'. It would also train the next generation to fill 'the high offices of state'.[24]

Which of the competing British models of a university should New South Wales embrace? The need for a university was not self-evident to many in the colony; Wentworth and his allies had to frame a case that spoke convincingly to local concerns. Their solutions to a number of technical questions shaped not just the proposed University of Sydney, but the many Australian institutions that would follow.

It might be expected Wentworth would look to Cambridge, his alma mater. No doubt his experience there proved influential. Yet the Oxbridge model—'residential, tutorial, character-forming'[25]—did not translate well. Cambridge's association with the established church, its curriculum, residency requirement and physical distance from the capital embodied an approach ill-suited for colonial Sydney. So through 1849 and 1850, Wentworth and associates worked on an alternative model for an Australian university, one based in a city and more in tune with educational reformers keen to teach modern subjects to a wide audience.

In their study of dominion legacies, Sydney-based historians Julia Horne and Geoffrey Sherington suggest that Australia's first universities embodied three fundamental values about the nature of public institutions: they should not be beholden to religious beliefs; access should be decided by merit alone, tested through public examination; and financial support should come not just from government but from public-spirited citizens.[26] Merit would temper privilege.

Such values seem unremarkable today, but the University of Sydney was among the first established in the British world along such lines; it would take another half century before 'these beliefs had become the norm for most universities in the British Empire'.[27]

To understand the ideas underpinning the first university in Australia, it is helpful to trace how policy makers shaped the University of Sydney, for taken in aggregate the choices they embraced sum to the Australian idea of a university.

A public institution

Who should own and operate an Australian university? There seems little evidence the matter was much debated. Harvard and Yale provided familiar examples of private colleges in the United States, but Wentworth and his contemporaries looked only to British practice: the new university would be a public institution, established by government and funded with public money. It would levy fees on students but offer scholarships for deserving candidates who could not afford a place on campus.

Thus, a motion moved by Wentworth in the New South Wales Legislative Council on 28 June 1850 proposed a 'University for the promotion of Literature and Science', established with £5,000 per annum, provided at public expense.[28]

This public status meant the university would sit within the state, legally under the supervision—however nominal—of a minister and the oversight—however sporadic—of the parliament. It would be public in a legal sense, but public also as an institution of the society that called it into being, 'constituted and shaped by political projects and the broader settlements that underpin them'.[29] *Public* ownership remains the norm; to this day, 97 per cent of degrees awarded in Australia are provided by universities established by legislation and owned by a state, territory or federal government.[30]

A self-governing institution

Britain could call on a ready-made instrument for constituting a public university. The Royal Charter provided a template for internal governance and a legal guarantee of independence for universities. Although the Royal Charter was not available for Australian colonies, they could pass legislation to achieve the same end, creating the new University of Sydney as a statutory entity with its own governing council, supported financially but not controlled by government.

Legislation establishing the University of Sydney passed in 1850, and the new institution was proclaimed in the *New South Wales Government Gazette*. A senate, initially comprising sixteen appointed fellows, would govern the institution. Only men were appointed, with educational backgrounds richly suggestive of the mix of influences underpinning the first Australian university—five foundation fellows had no university education, five were Cambridge graduates and one had graduated from Oxford. Three had attended Trinity College Dublin and two had attended Edinburgh.[31]

The Act established the University of Sydney as a 'body politic and corporate' with perpetual succession, able to make its own statutes within the broader Act of Parliament.[32] This made the university *self-governing*, though in a different sense from Oxbridge. The new institution would be overseen not by a collegium of academics answerable only to themselves, but by a board of supervisors appointed by legislators. Over time, this arrangement would produce lively tensions between governance and professorial expectations of independence. After serving as an externally appointed part-time vice-chancellor at the University of Melbourne, an exasperated Sir John Monash declared he found it easier to organise an army on the Western Front than to run a university.[33]

Still, such arguments occurred within the institution; Australian universities, from the first, operated with an expectation of significant autonomy from government, despite their reliance on public funding. Again, this model has endured, with nineteenth-century governance arrangements still largely intact.

A university of professional courses

Universities inspire lofty rhetoric. Proponents suggested the new University of Sydney would produce 'a long

line of illustrious names—of statesmen—of patriots—
of philanthropists—of philosophers—of poets—and of
heroes—who would shed a deathless halo, not only on
their country, but upon that University which called them
into being'.[34]

The deathless halo of fame notwithstanding, there
were practical considerations to resolve. A degree of
public funding implied useful returns to the colony, such
as addressing the shortage of skilled professionals. This
created an immediate tension with the Oxbridge model
of education. With a focus on the literary, philosophical
and mathematical 'greats' of the western canon, the
curriculum of Oxford and Cambridge did not speak to
the practical needs of colonial Sydney.

Hence, the founding statute of the University of
Sydney looked forward to *professional education*, with
specific mentions of law, medicine, pharmacy, surgery
and midwifery.[35] As historian Richard Selleck observes,
the colonies would need 'mining and construction engineers, surveyors, botanists, chemists, agriculturists,
astronomers, legislators, geologists, physicians, surgeons,
teachers, journalists, lawyers, judges'.[36] The new institution was expected to educate the professional classes
of Sydney.

The preference for professional degrees was somewhat
tempered by broader aspirations. The first principal at
Sydney, John Woolley, was a classicist, keen to see students benefit from a liberal arts education.[37] Professional
disciplines such as law and medicine were recognised by
the university from its foundation, but did not become
teaching faculties for some decades. The first undergraduates at Sydney were required to study in an arts degree
for a year or more before passing on to professional

qualifications. Exam papers from 1880, still available in the University of Sydney calendar archives, offer copious prose and verse to be translated into Latin and Greek.

Yet student preference for professional qualifications over generalist degrees arose early and proved insistent. Direct enrolment in professional courses became the established pattern at Sydney by the 1880s, and soon accounted for around 70 per cent of students. This number would move little over the next hundred years.[38]

A meritocratic institution

Speaking to his proposal for a University of Sydney, William Wentworth declared the institution would allow 'the child of every class, to become great and useful in the destinies of this country'.[39] Here was merit understood in two senses—economic, so that class should not be a barrier to participation, and social, relating to distinction of religion. Wentworth did not consider merit in a third sense, that of equality of opportunity for women.

In their influential study on the original educational franchise in Australia, Horne and Sherington document the success of opening tertiary education to a wide constituency. They stress the importance of a scholarship scheme as 'central to the meritocratic aims' of the institution. Paid by government, an annual scholarship of £50 supported around a third of students.[40] There was no means test, just an examination, with a majority of scholarships won by students from outside the traditional educated classes of the clergy, law and professions.

A *meritocratic* institution mirrored broader colonial sentiment—that of a place aspiring to avoid the class distinctions of British society. It would be a society where the son of a convict could become a distinguished legislator, and the hard-working find themselves studying at university.

Entry to university on merit also spoke to a second issue, the role of religion. The Oxbridge approach to higher education presented Australian legislators with an insuperable political problem—close links between the ancient universities and the established Anglican church.[41] This made the model unacceptable in a colonial society riven by sectarian tensions. For Wentworth, an Australian university must be 'open to all, though influenced by none'.[42]

The idea of a university on the basis of academic distinction alone, without reference to religious conviction, may seem self-evident, but it was a contested concept in the Sydney of 1850. The precedent had been set by London University and the Scottish institutions, but religious leaders in New South Wales objected vigorously to the secular constitution for the new university proposed by Wentworth. Legislative Council debate focused on the 'historical basis of religion at the centre of a university'.[43] Though the university was to 'teach secular knowledge', suggests historian Alan Atkinson, 'it did not follow that it was to be a secular institution'.[44] Legislators assumed a Christian character for the colony, and Wentworth talked of the new university 'proving the divinity of the great Christian code' and training minds that 'trusted and relied' upon that code.[45]

The religious imagination ran deep. The Great Hall at the University included carvings of angels and scrolls with Christian messages. A visitor felt that he 'gained in health and spirit, gazing at the beauty of its walls'.[46] Yet in practice, sectarian divisions and the absence of an established church in the Australian colonies made any specific spiritual affiliation unworkable. Whatever their underlying assumptions about pervasive Christian values, legislators established a secular institution in name and operation; the founding statute required that 'no religious test shall be administered' to any student or staff member at the University of Sydney.[47]

The legislative provision for an open educational franchise required students be selected by public examination, with a bursary system for those unable to afford the fees. An early success of the university was to admit Catholics and non-conformists in numbers that reflected their portion of the population.[48]

In time, the absence of religion shaped acceptable language about the purpose of the new institution. This would be a utilitarian institution befitting a pragmatic society. It was devoid of a chapel; its workaday discourse was not mantled in appeals to God; there was no evocation of campus life as resonant with moral purpose. Likewise missing were American campus tropes about university forming moral character and instilling the virtues necessary for democracy. In its origin, the Australian university was determinedly prosaic.

A commuter institution

As legislators pondered expectations of religious involvement in tertiary education, they hit upon a compromise: the university would be secular but welcome affiliated colleges with a religious character. Land was set aside for colleges to provide 'residence, religious teaching and tutorial assistance'.[49] In 1861, only two students at the University of Sydney lived on campus, though by 1900 this figure grew to around 15 per cent of the student body. Some colleges began with plentiful resources, but for others 'money was scarce, building slow, students few'.[50] Staff could be unreliable—the first permanent warden of St Paul's College was dismissed in 1861 'after he had been seen in an inebriated state on a Manly ferry'.[51]

By contracting religious instruction to residential colleges, legislators defined the meritocratic character of the first and subsequent public universities. This decision bore unforeseen consequences. Colleges were not the financial responsibility of the university, and ambitious early plans stalled for want of finance. Churches had more pressing priorities, and it was years before the first colleges opened. This was particularly acute for women. Though women were admitted to all degrees at the University of Adelaide from 1880, the first Australian institution to do so, there was only temporary accommodation in a cottage for female students from 1916.[52] Not until 1947 did the University open St Ann's College for women.

With modest opportunities to reside on campus, students made other arrangements. They lived at home or in lodgings, making Australian universities *commuter* institutions, places for local students to study during the day. Universities remain so. Though some institutions now host significant numbers in colleges and halls of residence, only around 5 per cent of Australian university students reside on campus during their degree program.[53] A commuter campus has implications for student life, with students disappearing into the surrounding city at the end of classes. Early observers noted the lack of social and political life; outside teaching times, campus could be a lonely and desolate place. More recently, the necessity of part-time work for many students undercuts campus life even during semester.

The non-residential nature of Australian universities has also influenced internal governance. In the ancient universities of the United Kingdom, colleges often pre-dated the university, and remained an essential part of its teaching and governance. In Australia, the universities were founded afresh as unitary institutions, single entities that could host colleges but not be beholden to them.

A comprehensive institution

The University of Sydney was assumed to be *comprehensive*, in the sense of covering the widest possible array of academic disciplines. Securing disciplinary coverage proved a project of many decades, but helped define the Australian university. A comprehensive institution made sense in a continent with only a few cities, far apart, and only one university in each city.

Like the QWERTY keyboard, the comprehensive character of Australian tertiary institutions remains entrenched even after the original logic has vanished. There are now Australian cities with five or six public universities, yet still only modest specialisation among institutions. Medical schools remain strictly rationed by government, but otherwise curriculum offerings are remarkably uniform. Most Australian public universities offer courses in science and arts, engineering and business. Many provide nursing (only the ANU, Macquarie and UNSW abstain). Just one public university, Federation, does not offer a law degree, though it provides law subjects as part of a business degree.

The assumption that public tertiary institutions should be comprehensive, even in crowded markets, has been part of the Australian idea of a university for as long as universities could choose their own profile. In this,

Australian practice has anticipated international developments, with the comprehensive university now dominant
in many education systems.[54]

Teaching and research

A standard model does not imply a static, stable world.
On the contrary, universities can be places of lively argument about the curriculum, and about student and staff
behaviour. Heated debates on governing boards find
their way into the metropolitan media. New areas of
study prove controversial, with long arguments about
whether dentistry or nursing, media studies or creative
writing deserve a place on campus.

The first Australian university defined its mission
around teaching. By-laws at the University of Sydney
required daily lectures during term, each of one hour, by
the professors of classics, mathematics and experimental
physics. These were scheduled between 9 a.m. and 1 p.m.,
Monday to Saturday. Some subjects were popular with
students, others languished. Early classes in jurisprudence
attracted large crowds at Sydney, earning the lecturer
backhanded encouragement from the senate. He should
make his classes 'as popular as lectures on jurisprudence
were likely to be, without making them unworthy of the
University'.[55] By contrast, the original course in German
at the University of Sydney was abandoned when the
single enrolled student quit the class.

Though the university saw itself as embodying new
thinking about higher education, for some it could never
be contemporary enough. A letter to the *Sydney Morning
Herald* in November 1857—just a few years after the
first classes on campus—complained of a curriculum that
was 'at the very best *ten years behind the age* in which

we are living'. It was time, suggested the writer, for more contemporary subjects in the humanities, medicine and physical sciences.[56]

An exclusive focus on teaching as the sole mission of the university altered only slowly. Any inclusion of research in the university mission was resisted strongly at first. The original Australian universities reflected conventional British wisdom that teaching is the principal occupation for a scholar. In 1755, Dr Samuel Johnson's *Dictionary* defined a university as 'a school where all the arts and faculties are taught'. A century later, John Henry Newman strongly opposed any place for research in a true university. For him, a university was a 'place of teaching university knowledge', where 'rashness is rendered innocuous, and error exposed, by the collision of mind with mind, and knowledge with knowledge'. In such a setting, teachers are too busy to do research, and researchers too preoccupied to teach. Indeed, said Newman, 'If its object were scientific and philosophical discovery, I do not see why a University should have students'.[57]

This emphasis on teaching appealed strongly to colonial governments, keen to secure graduates for the professions. Professor John Woolley, an Oxford graduate, used his inaugural address at the University of Sydney to define a university as a school for liberal and general knowledge and a collection of special colleges, devoted to the learned professions. He did not mention research. In 1878, Charles Pearson, a member of the Council of the University of Melbourne, asserted that the main function of a university professor was to 'impart, not invent'.

A determined defence of teaching allowed local educators and legislators to resist the growing influence of non-British perspectives on the mission of a university. In 1809, Prussian scholar and administrator Wilhelm von Humboldt proposed a new university in Berlin that combined education and research, making fundamental inquiry the work of a university professor. Humboldt talked of an intellectual institution to cultivate 'science and scholarship in the deepest and broadest sense'.[58] The campus would unite teaching and research as a single undertaking, with teachers who could share their discoveries with students, and demonstrate first-hand how new knowledge emerges.

Though absent at the founding of Australian tertiary education, the idea that research deserved a place alongside teaching eventually found adherents. Research laboratories began to appear on the Australian campus from the 1870s, though the idea of a research qualification as essential for an academic career remained controversial. A program of doctoral education was not offered in Australia until 1946. Some continued to argue for the 'mastery' of a discipline in the British research masters tradition as 'the longer, harder and more important route to expertise than the "horribly American" PhD, which privileged mere discovery of something new'.[59]

Given this opposition, it took decades to graft a research mission onto the original Australian idea of a university. Yet, eventually, this showed itself to be a significant development on campus and beyond. Universities would provide not just graduates, but some of the technical and medical breakthroughs necessary for contemporary life. Historian Geoffrey Blainey suggests that the introduction of research contributed to social acceptance, the 'growing idea that a university is perhaps not an extravagance'.[60]

Australia may have begun with teaching institutions, but in time the important technological innovations of German and American institutions, and a rising international interest in scientific research, became decisive. Research would become a universal attribute of Australian higher education, adopted by every institution and eventually required by law in the very definition of a university. It would prompt criticism of universities also, claims that academics are too preoccupied with research to value their students. The Humboldtian ideal of research influencing the classroom was challenged by growing division between the two activities, and by the emergence of specialist research-only posts. Achieving balance between *research* and *teaching* remains controversial on campus—even as both pursuits remain firmly within the accepted idea of a university.

THE PATH BEGINS

From inception, the University of Sydney borrowed curriculum and ethos from British practice. As in London, the university offered entry without religious qualification to those who passed an examination.[61] Classes were organised around the 'lecture and tutorial' model familiar in Scotland and Ireland, and the university employed professors, not tutors, as principal teachers. The university opened to those who could meet admissions standards, and supported through scholarships students who might struggle financially. Again, as at the University of London, students typically lived at home and travelled to campus for classes. Australia followed recently founded British and Irish universities in developing strong professional programs in medicine, law and engineering.

Yet, as Horne and Sherington have argued, the new institution also departed from British practice. The emphasis on merit for entry 'was an idea first successfully implemented in Australia and a hallmark of Australian universities from their foundation, part of the social contract between colonists and the government'.[62] Though the new institution featured architectural hints of the ancient universities in its design, and adopted a motto—*sidere mens eadem mutato*—to stress continuity with British origins,[63] it relied also on local invention in a colony many months' sailing from the mother country. A coat of arms featuring a familiar book under the Southern Cross neatly positioned the fledgling university.

This amalgam of British inheritance and Australian innovation was not a replica of any one British institution, but a response to the needs of urban Sydney and the aspirations of a local elite. The path invented for the nation's first metropolitan institution would shape Australian higher education. It proved an enduring act of public policy—'Sydney became the model for all Australian universities'.[64]

In 1853, the University of Melbourne followed Sydney. The idea for a second university on the Australian continent grew in part from inter-colonial rivalry. Victoria had just separated from New South Wales, as Melbourne boomed following the discovery of gold.[65] Championed by Redmond Barry, a judge of the Supreme Court of Victoria and leading member of fledgling Melbourne society, the new university would add to the esteem and civility of a suddenly wealthy colony.

This new university was established swiftly. A Bill was considered by the Legislative Council in January 1853, and received royal assent within weeks. The foundation Council for the University, announced by Lieutenant-Governor Charles La Trobe in April 1853, was populated once more with graduates from Oxford, Cambridge, Trinity and Edinburgh. As in Sydney, the founders selected a coat of arms invoking European wisdom under new skies. To teach the handful of men who would begin classes in April 1855, the new institution recruited four professors to cover mathematics, classics, natural sciences and modern history.

In Melbourne, those appointed to govern were drawn from the professions. Clerics were few, though the Council adopted an ecumenical approach by inviting the Anglican and Catholic bishops of Melbourne to join the governing body. Even so, Melbourne followed London University in excluding religious instruction from the curriculum.

The Act to establish the University of Melbourne required that the institution be 'open to all classes and denominations of Her Majesty's subjects'. As in Sydney, the new university would be a state-initiated entity, publicly owned and required to report to parliament each year.[66] In time, the new university would become known to its students as 'the shop'—an affectionate if matter-of-fact-description of an institution where students commuted to campus each day and studied for future careers.

There were subtle but significant differences between the newly established entities. Lectures were not compulsory at Melbourne; though most students were drawn from the 'urban middle classes', the University sought also to welcome students who had to work for a living and could study only in the evening.[67] Government was less generous with initial funding than in New South

Wales, making the new university more dependent on philanthropy, and perhaps more eager to offer professional courses that attracted enrolments.[68] Those founding the University of Melbourne would choose more austere architecture—sombre Scottish ecclesiastical stonework as against the exuberant gothic revival of Sydney's main quadrangle. Legislation differed in detail, and Melbourne moved with greater speed to create vocational faculties, with law (1857), engineering (1861) and medicine (1862) all operating within a decade of Charles La Trobe's laying a (now lost) brass plaque to begin the university.

As in Sydney, the educational franchise stressed merit selection. Horne and Sherington observe:

> The social contract in Australia was thus developed as a form of educational franchise first granted to urban males principally of middle-class background, but of diverse social and religious origins, and then increasingly extended to those in the emerging public school system, those of rural and regional background, and ultimately women. Much of this change had occurred by the 1880s.[69]

Those who found a place at the new university seemed determined to enjoy the experience. Students at Melbourne embraced the quaint rituals of university life, throwing each other into the lake or braving the £2 fine for plucking a camellia on campus.[70] University lecturers could incline to the eccentric. The first professor of mathematics at Melbourne, William Wilson, would sit in the lecture room 'watch in hand, calling the roll punctually whether or not the students had arrived'. He would then deliver his lecture to an empty room, 'marking it down as a source of examination questions'.[71]

Women appeared in classrooms at the University of Melbourne within two decades of foundation, though initially excluded from medical study. From 1887 all degrees at Melbourne, including medicine, were open to female students, though recruitment of women as academics proved fraught. The barriers to female careers on campus 'remained severe. In 1932, the percentage of professors who were women in Australian universities was zero'.[72] By this time, women accounted for more than a quarter of students on campus.

First Australians were also notably absent. The first recorded graduation of an Indigenous student in Australia was not until 1959, when Margaret Williams-Weir of the Malera and Bandjalang people of northern New South Wales completed her Diploma in Physical Education at the University of Melbourne. She would continue studying and teaching through a long and distinguished life, eventually earning a doctorate at the University of New England.[73]

Taken overall, the governance, funding and social impact of Australia's first two universities were strikingly similar. The new universities reflected analogous influences and adopted a similar organisational form and mission. In turn, they would inspire the next generation of institutions. The Province of South Australia established the University of Adelaide in 1874, using the same model. The Act of incorporation for the University of Adelaide mimicked key tenets from legislation in Sydney and Melbourne, creating a non-sectarian institution governed by an independent council empowered to award degrees. It embraced lofty language. The University of Adelaide, its first chancellor promised in 1877, would form the 'character of the governing classes' and 'help elevate the middle class to higher civilisation'.[74] The curriculum choices on offer, though, were similar to those operating in Sydney and Melbourne.

Hobart gained a university in 1890. The founders praised the 'no frills' Scottish model of university education, with instruction in the classroom rather than in Oxbridge-style colleges.[75] Brisbane followed in 1909, when the Queensland Government agreed to spend £10,000 a year for seven years to hire four professors and ten lecturers who would start a new university. Founding legislation drew once again on experience at the University of Sydney, even naming the governing body a 'senate', as in Sydney.[76] Two years later Perth welcomed the new University of Western Australia, with a strong commitment to practical and accessible courses. It would prove a place equally of serious scholarship and lively pranks—engineering students once drove a flock of sheep into Winthrop Hall to protest against the 'automated ritual of graduation ceremonies'.[77]

Each university was established by an Act of Parliament based on the now-dominant Australian model. In each case, land and funding supplied by the state would support a non-sectarian and self-governing institution. Though residential colleges would be established in due course, most students would commute to campus, complete a single undergraduate degree and leave for a life in the professions. The facts are unremarkable, yet each decision helped define a model that endures. Time present and time past point to time future.

A familiar pattern began early and has continued through generations.

THE METROPOLITAN IDEA

The Australian idea of the university arose in an urban setting and remains *metropolitan* in character—a campus in the city, focused on educating local students into the professions, tied to the life of the surrounding town. Australia would go on to develop universities in regional centres, though these would resemble their city cousins in outlook, curriculum and organisation. The path, once trod, continued to speak to Australian values, and to provide a comfortable logic. The prevailing model can seem natural; we forget this is just one of many possible tracks into the future.

That journey began with the University of Sydney and led quickly to similar undertakings in each colonial capital city. As a history of the University of Adelaide notes, Australians drew lessons from British models but tailored local institutions to the 'environmental and social characteristics' of new settlements. 'Thus developed a distinctly Australian tertiary system, with an eye for the Old Country.'[78]

The form was fixed early; by the 1860s, the senate at the University of Sydney, under the guiding hand of Principal Woolley, had 'set the pattern which later advocates of change would find difficult to overturn'.[79] Here was an enduring adaptation of British antecedents to local conditions, a series of choices that sum to an Australian approach. Historian Richard Selleck described the unique complexion of the new institutions:

> A state university, urban, secular, professorial, nonresidential and noncollegiate, centralised in government, controlled by a laity, and possessing power to teach and examine. Other universities had some of these characteristics, but none had this particular combination.[80]

This has been a journey, though not to a destination—for the model continues to evolve. A time would come when institutions, having looked beyond British models, found much to like in German research, European community engagement, American philanthropy. A set of secondary characteristics, though not mentioned at foundation, would eventually cluster around campus—expectations of academic freedom, a space for political activism, student newspapers to challenge censorship and the administration.[81] As historian Sheldon Rothblatt argues in a study of British universities, the idea of higher education is not fixed or coherent but arises by 'joining principles and values that at bottom have different historical origins and acutely different cultural meanings and purposes'.[82] The Australian experience embodies this accretion of ideas and aspirations, held together by a shared belief in education and research.

This rich array of ambitions is found in the mission statements of Australian universities. There are elements of Newman's insistence on teaching and intellectual formation, Humboldt's focus on advancing knowledge, the elite technical training of the French *grandes écoles*, mingled with more recent language about industry partnerships. Despite this accumulation of ideas, though, the typical Australian university is fundamentally similar to its neighbours, an expression of a shared national idea. A single path, beginning with a decision by the New South Wales legislature in 1850, has delivered a model of the university across a continent.

3

ATTEMPTS TO LEAVE THE PATH

The opening wave of universities in Australia ran from foundation of the University of Sydney in 1850 to 1913, when the first students commenced classes in Perth. By then, every state capital city hosted a university, each an expression of the standard Australian metropolitan model. The ideal type was self-replicating: each entity in this collection of institutions was publicly owned, self-governing, focused on professional degrees, meritocratic and non-residential, with a curriculum that aspired to the comprehensive. The first Australian universities would trace a common course, growing from small teaching to large research-based undertakings.

As the model completed its journey across the continent, the first murmurs about greater diversity surfaced. There were calls for further institutions in Sydney and Melbourne, campaigns for regional universities and advocates for a national university based in Canberra. Policy makers grasped that Australia had developed a narrow and exclusively urban model, and sought more choice for students. Their efforts would deliver an expanded number of universities and a more generous geographical spread, but no lively pluralism of institutional types.

Since the nineteenth century, regional voices have sought tertiary education beyond the capital cities. Country centres, too, needed graduates in the professions. Accordingly, some sought to provide opportunities for study far from state capitals. Between the two world wars of the twentieth century, this regional aspiration found embodiment in the Northern Tablelands of New South Wales.

In 1892, Armidale Mayor William Drew boasted that his city had already become a centre for school education. In time, he suggested, Armidale could host a university like Oxford. A teacher's college arrived in 1929, and on New Year's Day 1938 Armidale welcomed a 'northern university' with the foundation of the New England University College. The college would be affiliated with the University of Sydney, and draw on its parent for curriculum, organisational design and governance. It worked with this arrangement until accredited as an independent university on 1 February 1954. The birth of the new institution, reported lecturer in classics Frank Letters, was heralded when 'one minute after midnight' a stream of meteors 'soared across the sky between the Big Dipper and the Southern Cross'.

This first Australian university outside a capital city established itself as a respected institution within a prosperous rural setting. Importantly, it pioneered distance-education options, an expression of its commit-ment to make tertiary education more widely available. The success of the University of New England (UNE) argued the case for more tertiary institutions outside cap-ital cities, with residential life on campus and academic specialisations aligned to local industry. Yet the form of the institution owed much to the standard Australian idea of a university, aspiring to comprehensive offerings and research. As UNE developed, reports its jubilee his-tory, the 'regional location (and obligations) became a less prominent feature of its identity'.[1]

While the University of Sydney provided the tem-plate for New England, from 1951 the New South Wales University of Technology (as UNSW was then titled) supported tertiary campuses with a technical focus. The government of New South Wales was keen to increase the supply of 'engineers, metallurgists and chemists. An essential element of this plan was the establishment of University Divisions in the steel and mining towns of Wollongong, Newcastle and Broken Hill'.

Once again, demand for trained professionals prompted new universities, though local sentiment argued for broad institutions rather than technical schools. In Wollongong, the manager of the steel works, Gus Parish, urged the addition of arts and commerce to a univer-sity college dominated by engineering. In Newcastle, this same message was voiced by Anglican Bishop Francis de Witt Bailey, a graduate of Balliol College, Oxford. The addition of arts, he reasoned, would make Newcastle a 'proper' university.[2]

These new campuses thrived, with Newcastle awarded full university status in 1965 and Wollongong a decade later. Each served its community with distinction, developing over time the familiar array of faculties and degrees offered by an Australian public university. The enterprise at Broken Hill was less successful, whittling down the range of offerings until just mining remained. In 1981, the Council of the University of New South Wales resolved to close the division, with the final students graduating four years later.[3]

The pattern of satellite campuses graduating into full universities recurred in centres across the nation. In 1959, the Parliament of Queensland debated a new university in the tropics. A key theme was the cost for regional students moving to Brisbane for tertiary study. Minister for Education, Jack Pizzey, talked about giving 'northern students in science and engineering' an opportunity to do at least their first year of study in Townsville. From 1960, a new campus of the University of Queensland in Townsville provided the base for James Cook University, which would issue degrees in its own right from 1970.

Minister Pizzey predicted that investing in Far North Queensland would prompt 'pressure from Central Queensland to establish a centre in Rockhampton'.[4] The Queensland Institute of Technology (Capricornia) was founded in 1967. It became the University of Central Queensland in 1992.

As new universities spun out from established players, they transplanted to new communities an existing metropolitan mode of education and organisation. Though vast distances separated these fledgling institutions, the campus layout, curriculum and internal governance proved familiar—these were proud colonies rather than bold new departures.

The vision for an Australian capital, articulated at federation, assumed a national university. In 1930, the new capital of Canberra acquired a small institution. The Canberra University College, supported by the University of Melbourne, offered part-time classes after hours at Telopea Park School. With a prominent site for a future university included in the original plans for the national capital, a small after-hours tertiary program would never suffice.

The idea of a national university allowed proponents to recommend a thoroughgoing departure from the standard model. Alternatives proposed included American research institutions such as Johns Hopkins in Baltimore, which focused on high-quality research. The national university should likewise be a research institution with no undergraduate teaching—and hence unlike existing Australian institutions.[5]

The creation of an Australian national university would be delayed by economic depression, war and wider uncertainty about the future of Canberra. Not until 1944 would a substantive proposal for the university be complete. This called for a disciplinary focus on government and policy studies, history and literature. A concurrent proposal for a national medical research institute was championed by Nobel Laureate Howard Florey, while Sir Mark Oliphant pressed for a strong campus presence for physics.[6]

In 1946, the Commonwealth legislated to create the Australian National University (ANU). Here was difference—formulated, planned and, for a while, honoured in the implementation. The new institution would pursue a mission to 'encourage, and provide facilities for, postgraduate research and study, both generally and in relation to subjects of national importance to Australia'.[7] Nugget Coombs, a member of the university's Interim

Council, finished a planning meeting by seeking reassurance that everyone understood the departure from standard Australian practice. 'We are all happy, are we,' he asked, 'that it will be a full research university?'[8] The founding Act established research schools in medicine, physical sciences, social sciences and Pacific studies.

This first iteration of the ANU lasted less than fifteen years. In 1960, the institution was merged with the undergraduate Canberra University College. The newly expanded ANU acquired the familiar undergraduate arts, science and professional programs found in other Australian universities, though the separation of research schools and faculties persisted for a further quarter century. 'Although the ANU was unique,' as the history commissioned for its fiftieth anniversary opined, 'the broad structure of its government was the same as other Australian universities, which in turn had drawn on British models.'[9]

Subsequent choices diminished further the special status of the ANU. It surrendered some dedicated funding to compete in national research schemes and became subject to the same federal government rules and regimes that governed other Australian universities. When existing Australian universities embraced postgraduate training in the 1940s, they rendered redundant the unique mission of a national facility in Canberra. With time's passage, the specialist mission that animated the original ANU design was lost to the more familiar model—a public research university focused on professional degrees, with a teaching curriculum that aspired to the comprehensive. The ANU still enjoys exclusive access to a National Institute Grant, but in other respects it has joined the mainstream of Australian higher education.

THE SECOND WAVE OF INSTITUTIONS

The University of New England and ANU were amongst the first to create new institutions with a unique mission. During the long economic boom following World War II, science and technology became policy priorities. Politicians talked of specialist universities to train scientists, technicians and engineers for national prosperity.

The New South Wales University of Technology was the first commitment to a tertiary institution with an explicit science and technology character. Technical education in Australia stretched back to the foundation of the Sydney Mechanics Institute in 1843 and the formation of the Sydney Technical College in 1878. A new university would develop this tradition in the eastern suburbs of Sydney—even if a patronising editorial in the *Sydney Morning Herald* welcomed a new institution to take on extensive teaching so that the University of Sydney could better focus on original research.

The *Technical Education and New South Wales University of Technology Act 1949* established the new institution designed to provide specialist training 'in the various branches of technology and science', paying attention to 'their application to industry and commerce'. Research would have an industrial focus.[10] This was a new model for a technical university for Australia, carefully guided by first Vice-Chancellor Sir Philip Baxter.

As with the ANU, the new institution retained many of its founding features but merged quickly into the wider Australian university tradition. The exclusive focus on science and technology lasted only briefly. In 1957, the Murray Report to the Commonwealth proposed that the fledging university 'be widened to include arts and medical studies and that its name be changed to the University of New South Wales'.[11] With these changes, noted Murray, 'it must be expected that the N.S.W. University of Technology will assume many of the features of a traditional university'.[12] So it came to pass. With a new name and expanded faculties, including arts, medicine and law, a distinctive original mission for UNSW was replaced by a familiar comprehensive profile.[13]

Victoria could call on a strong tradition of technical education, and seemed better placed to create a technical university. Amid reports that the University of Melbourne was 'bursting at its seams',[14] the state government embraced the idea of a new institution with a proposal to convert the long-established Royal Melbourne Technical College into a university. The idea faced political and bureaucratic opposition. As Member for Albert Park, Keith Sutton, told the Victorian Parliament, 'I could never quite rid my mind of the disturbing thought that the words "University of Technology" or "Technical University" involved a contradiction in terms'.[15] He urged instead the establishment of an institution focused on 'the pursuit and passing on of wide general knowledge and for research animated by a passion for truth'.

More tellingly, the Victorian government department in charge of technical education had no interest in surrendering its flagship institution. Attention then shifted to the idea of a new university, located on a greenfield site south-east of the city. As in Sydney, the Victorian Government proposed that a second university be organised around science and technology. The Murray Report disagreed, claiming that a wider offering was more desirable because the incorporation of arts, law and psychology 'would be essential for the intellectual health of the new institution'.[16]

On 13 March 1961, the first 347 students commenced studies at the Monash University campus in suburban Clayton. The institution grew quickly, adding the
professional faculties found in longer-established universities. By 1966, Monash was teaching over 6,000 students across a wide array of disciplines. Though strong
in science and engineering, as originally promised,
Monash became another comprehensive institution in the
Australian mould. As Foundation Professor John Legge
declared on the fifteenth anniversary of the institution,
'having seen itself in 1960 as the first of the new universities', Monash 'succeeded, maybe, in establishing itself as
the last of the old'.[17]

The lack of significant differentiation disappointed
many who championed a distinctive approach. At a 1965
seminar on the future of higher education, the first vice-
chancellor of Monash, JAL Matheson, was reported
as saying, 'I speak … as one who has tried—who
indeed came to this country with the avowed intention
of trying—to produce a university different in character
from the other university in the city in which Monash is
located. Instead of this I now find myself vice-chancellor
of a University that is disappointingly like the University
of Melbourne'.

There are, of course, worse disappointments in life.

At both UNSW and Monash, plans for specialisation in science and technology were overtaken by urgent
demand from government and students for the full array
of professional faculties found in existing universities.
This was achieved with impressive results, but the original aspiration to difference was not sustained. The ANU,
UNSW and Monash would, by turns, come to resemble the established archetype of an Australian university,

with organisation, courses and academic mission similar
to those found at Sydney and Melbourne. Only the architecture remained genuinely different.

DIVERSITY AND A THIRD WAVE OF NEW UNIVERSITIES

The 1960s are remembered as a time of student protest
and dissent on campus. The program of Orientation
Week talks on the ANU campus for 1969 invited students to consider tanks and freedom in Czechoslovakia,
student revolt, a republic for New Guinea and the value
of marching. Should the Berlin crisis blow up during the
week, noted the program, 'the 3.00–4.00 pm time slot
will be used for an expert talk or debate on this topic'.[18]

At Monash, 'the troubles' lasted from 1967 to
1974. As historians Graeme Davison and Kate Murphy
observe, 'the times were revolutionary'.[19] The journal of
the National Civic Council, *News Weekly*, described the
university as the 'Monash Soviet' with 'more subversion
per square foot than at any other Australian university'.[20]

The growth of student activism fostered cultural,
political and social change. Clive James recalled the
intensity of language around new verse, new arguments—
'I was so excited that my badges rattled. There were
sparks coming off my lapel'.[21] Change could also pro-
voke divisions. At a seminar at the ANU on 'The Future
of Universities', an academic asked why these institutions were becoming unpopular with parents, especially
when students were the first from their family to study.
'Because,' explained Professor Don Anderson, 'we take
their kids away for three or four years, and when we have
finished with them they can't talk to each other.'[22]

The times inspired a mood for change, including change in institutional design. In Britain, the 1963

Robbins Report recommended the establishment of new universities and encouraged experiment and innovation. Australia likewise experienced similar rapid growth in student numbers, with a sustained burst of new institutions. This began with Macquarie in 1964, and within less than twenty years included La Trobe, Newcastle, Wollongong, Griffith, Deakin and Murdoch. Here, once again, was a chance to break the mould and create something new.

For many new institutions, the great organising principle would be interdisciplinarity—bringing down the walls between academic fields, thereby enabling students to range across the full spectrum of human knowledge. Interdisciplinarity encouraged curricular innovation and new ways to organise academic life. Interdisciplinarity would open a new way ahead, and so end the dominance of a single idea of the Australian university. The emerging universities could embrace fields not supported in older universities, and make their name with original contributions to the study of Asia, the environment, the humanities and culture. Vice-Chancellor David Derham at Melbourne might explain that his institution avoided student radicalism because it did not teach sociology,[23] but elsewhere academics and students were keen to embrace the restlessness of the times.

A shortage of places on campus encouraged the first in a new wave of institutions: Macquarie University. Established as the third university in a city, it could be designed in conscious contrast to Sydney and UNSW. At a time of rising nationalism, the new university would be the first in the state named after a prominent Australian, with the New South Wales Cabinet debating whether to honour the architect of higher education William Wentworth, influential premier Sir Henry Parkes or early governor Lachlan Macquarie. As Bruce Mansfield and Mark Hutchinson aver in their history of the institution, there is irony in a place once described as 'Australia's most radical and unconventional university' carrying the name of a 'staunch Scots Tory and High Anglican soldier who had governed New South Wales at the height of the convict era'.[24]

For a motto, the founders turned to Chaucer rather than Latin, though 'And gladly teche' recalled an earlier era of higher education, since research was always part of the Macquarie mission. Still, founding Vice-Chancellor AG Mitchell was determined that Macquarie would be different. Instead of the usual choice of programs, Macquarie offered a single undergraduate degree to encourage breadth of study. It would stress access and participation, and seek links across academic disciplines. Unlike its city competitors, Macquarie would not be comprehensive but instead would develop distinctive areas of academic strength.

The new university chose an innovative structure to encourage academic cross-fertilisation. Rather than mobilising traditional disciplinary departments, Macquarie would organise itself as a single college, along the lines of American universities, encompassing the arts and sciences. The institution looked also to recent British innovations, such as the integrated first-year course proposed for Sussex University in Brighton. This inspired Fred Chong, Foundation Chair in Mathematics, to describe subject choice at Macquarie as 'an academic cafeteria'. A student might select a variety of titbits or 'a veritable feast on a few favoured dishes'.[25]

Even as they designed a distinctive approach, Macquarie pioneers acknowledged a risk that the institution would in time abandon difference and trek the familiar Australian path. Chancellor Percy Partridge voiced this concern during planning for the new university. Would Macquarie, he asked, 'be subject to the iron law of reversion to type?'[26] This concern has run through Macquarie's history, a worry that under pressure the institution would not hold its ground and defend a 'broad educational mission as tenaciously as it should'.[27]

Macquarie remains a flourishing institution with innovative programs, but it is no longer the outlier. Messages to potential undergraduate students stress breadth of offerings and freedom to explore, but in place of a single degree the Macquarie course guide offers dozens of degrees, from a Bachelor of Actuarial Studies to a Bachelor of Teaching (Early Childhood Education). The academic structure has migrated to the standard Australian organisation, with disciplinary departments grouped in faculties. Over its half a century of academic and community contribution, Macquarie has moved into the mainstream.

Flinders University in South Australia also provides an example of a university founded on aspirations to lower disciplinary walls.[28] The original plans called for a second campus for the University of Adelaide at Bedford Park. Academic appointments had already begun when a new state government embraced a more sweeping approach, a second university for the capital city.

The first Flinders students arrived in 1966. They were typical of their time. Men outnumbered women two to one. Most lived at home with their parents, their background overwhelmingly middle class. A survey in the first years of the new institution confirmed Flinders students were not politically radical. A slim majority indicated support for the government of Harold Holt. Only a handful opposed American and Australian involvement in Vietnam. If conservative about political change, the Flinders students did not forgo Commencement Day pranks, with a mock Russian submarine pushed into the university lake. Most students studying at Flinders were destined for teaching or the public service.

Though Flinders students were much like Australian tertiary students elsewhere, their new university was anything but typical. As founding Vice-Chancellor Peter Karmel told a meeting at the Adelaide Town Hall, 'we want to experiment and experiment bravely'.[29] Instead of traditional faculties and departments, there would be schools of Social Sciences, Biological Sciences, Physical Sciences, and Language and Literature. Students, it was hoped, would explore the spaces between disciplines, in a university committed to a coherent intellectual and social experience. Even when the university began to teach medicine in 1975, the course was designed so students would take majors in other faculties. Many chose the humanities and social sciences.

Innovation at Flinders extended from subject matter to teaching method. The School of Language and Literature introduced the novel practice of continuous assessment, with teaching delivered through now-unimaginable tutorials of just three or four students. Flinders students could take Australia's first undergraduate course in Spanish, along with other subjects not offered at the University of Adelaide.

With no God professors reigning over departments, Flinders staff were expected to contribute to leadership. A participatory system of government would prevail, in which decisions were taken, as David Hilliard's book on Flinders recounts, 'often at wearisome length'.[30] However exhausting, the approach created a sense of community among staff. Numbers were sufficiently small that everyone could know the vice-chancellor. Flinders recruited widely, with many young academics establishing families in a new city, and forming close bonds with each other and their new university.

Yet, as years passed, familiar patterns returned. What originated as radical departure began to take on the degree structures, teaching practice and governance fabric of Australian orthodoxy. Engineering began at Flinders in 1990, with law approved the same year. A review of administrative structures recommended the introduction of faculties, a semantic change acknowledging the pressure of rapid growth in enrolments and the need for better signalling of course offerings.[31]

Located away from the city centre, in what Premier Don Dunstan unkindly described as a 'suburban paddock', Flinders has retained many traces of its distinctive ethos, notably a character defined by difference from the University of Adelaide. However, in time Flinders responded to student preferences and to competition from the new University of South Australia by offering more professional qualifications. Interdisciplinarity became an aspiration rather than a thoroughgoing point of difference. What began as a brave experiment is now an institution firmly embedded within the Australian norm.

The story of La Trobe, which began operations in 1967 in the northern Melbourne suburb of Bundoora, traces a similar transformation over decades. Robert Manne joined a university 'without a vocational faculty' but watched the centre of gravity at La Trobe move slowly towards professional degrees. 'The moment I recognised something fundamental was shifting was when

Alpine Tourism appeared in a corridor of the Social Sciences building where I worked.'[32]

La Trobe graduate historian Don Watson makes clear his disappointment at this end to idealism:

> Two decades after La Trobe opened to students, much of the founders' philosophy had been forgotten. The college system had been scrapped; the school had been broken into departments; power had passed from the professors to administrators; governments were deciding the shape and function of the University and pushing it away from the original broad education model and towards greater specialisation and concentration; basic (scientific) research was being abandoned in favour of short-term, 'goal orientated' research, much of it determined by 'Procrustean politicians' perceptions of what is good for the country'.[33]

Yet the sense of creating something new was never lost entirely. La Trobe placed great emphasis on its humanities expertise, and has maintained this tradition. Perhaps more than other third-wave institutions, the transition to standard Australian curriculum and governance at La Trobe posed challenges to governance and management.

In the west, Murdoch too wrestled with tension between its original vision and pressures to conform, a trajectory that social scientist Toby Miller describes as 'from periphery to core' (and sometimes back to the periphery).[34] Murdoch began with innovative offerings such as a foundation veterinary science program, and added professional offerings along the way, including a law program from 1993. Named after the Foundation Professor of

English and later Chancellor of the University of Western Australia, Sir Walter Murdoch,[35] Perth's second university aimed to address knowledge with 'humane and vital intelligence'.[36]

The new university established itself as a place of both new ideas and practical cooperation. It put early students to work in a very practical sense, creating a new setting for tertiary education in Western Australia:

> During the early months of 1977 a large party of students and staff devoted themselves to digging out an amphitheatre on the western side of the campus which could be used for open-air performances. At the end of November it was used for the first time for a staging of *Toad of Toad Hall*.[37]

All institutions are unique, and yet alike: more than fifty years earlier, staff and students at the University of Western Australia likewise banded together to dig a reflection pond in front of Winthrop Hall.[38] The pond was finished just hours before the opening ceremony for the new building, and filled with water lilies that the university website concedes, tactfully, 'may or may not have been "borrowed" from Queens Gardens'.[39] Murdoch University pushed further, intellectually and organisationally. It proved inventive in other ways—an Orgone box was constructed in the common room of the School of Social Inquiry, and the staff choir at graduation ceremonies mustered uncommon virtuosity in singing a cantata based on the university's parking regulations.[40]

Murdoch worried about drifting too far from conventional practice. To secure students the university needed popular courses and recognisable degree titles.

It negotiates still the tensions between founding mission and contemporary expectations. Like other universities, Murdoch is a community both distinct and working within familiar structures and patterns. Institutions may nurture their own characters and aspirations, even as they converge organisationally.

As this last third-wave institution has moved towards the mainstream, the experience at Murdoch has underscored the episodic nature of innovation. Important social movements, notably feminism, made lasting changes on campus, but the brief flurry of interest in new organisational forms did not endure. Keen advocates of consultation councils and university assemblies graduated or moved to other interests. Energy around institutional difference evaporated as inherited forms quietly resumed their influence.

ACADEMIC CULTURE

Path dependency is not just a grand historical narrative but the cumulative choices of individuals. To endure over generations, universities must employ academics and professional staff with a commitment to their mission—people who honour a shared sense of what matters. They become the bearers of their institution's tradition, the colleagues who steer its destiny. When one road is preferred to the others that are available, this is not an assertion of some inevitable force. Human initiative is at work.

In particular, academic norms tally closely with institutional practice. Academic judgement is the basis of curriculum quality control, of access and appointment, of promotion and reward. Professors promote their own disciplines as suitable subjects for teaching, and resist encroachment from fields they consider unsuitable for a university. They share with peers in other places a sense of what is appropriate for a university, an understanding drawn from institutional practice elsewhere, and personal experience. Professional staff support and create structures to make the organisation work effectively. The university is not separate from its staff; it reflects the interaction of organisational form with the values and priorities of those who work within the gates.

Staff profiles have changed as the university mission has shifted. Through the twentieth century, and on to the present day, research has become ever more central to the university mission. This means teaching-focused staff have lost out to academics who combine teaching with research. A 1965 survey found 21 per cent of academic staff in Australia with teaching-only duties. By the 1990s, this number had declined to just 3.5 per cent.[41] As universities were standardised by national policy and prevailing academic culture, so the university workforce lost diversity of experience.

A brief personal account may illustrate how academics, as bearers of a tradition, reinforce a dominant model.

My first academic position was teaching public policy in the School of Social and Industrial Administration at Griffith University, then a small, single-campus institution in a forest south of Brisbane. The second university in the city, Griffith began teaching in 1975. Like other third-wave universities, Griffith embraced a fierce commitment to interdisciplinary education and a reputation for radical epistemology. When I applied for a lectureship a decade after the first student intake, prospective academic staff were required to write a short essay outlining their personal commitment to an interdisciplinary pedagogy.

Induction sessions for the successful applicants stressed this fundamental organising principle for the new institution.

As at Macquarie and Flinders, Griffith embraced schools not faculties, concentration areas rather than disciplinary departments, and degree structures that emphasised knowledge across domains. There were no professional degrees, and strict limits were placed on subjects offered by each academic concentration with the School of Social and Industrial Administration. This required students to range across numerous fields to complete a degree. Academic decisions were made in consultative committees by a young and enthusiastic staff keen to innovate. In his history of Griffith's early years, Noel Quirke observed that 'Australian Environmental Studies was so near the academic cutting edge in the early seventies that the primary challenge for its first Chairman, Professor Calvin Rose, was to determine what actually constituted the field of environmental studies'.[42]

This lively and argumentative culture attracted an early satirical novel. *Pushed From the Wings*, by Griffith academic Ross Fitzgerald, lampooned philosophers falling asleep amid heat and humidity while reading *The Death of Socrates*, students conspicuously carrying Trotsky's *The Permanent Revolution*, anarchist teaching fellows with private incomes, and a self-imposed tyranny of the collective.[43] We could guess the identity of familiar colleagues working in the humanities.

Griffith was a determined effort to break with existing practice. But where to hire for such an enterprise? The university recruited some superb international academics, a sprinkling of new doctoral graduates such as myself, and many local academics from existing institutions. For some recruits Griffith was a chance to experiment, but for others it proved a disappointing shadow of the 'real university' just across the river. At the nearby University of Queensland, one could find comforting tradition in sandstone buildings housing professional faculties and disciplinary departments, recognisable degrees and a decision-making process easier to navigate than the sometimes baffling democratic processes of the Nathan campus.

As a young academic, I joined a university constantly torn between those committed to Griffith's founding mission, and those anxious (even if unconsciously) to recreate the University of Queensland in a new setting. The touch points were the radical edges of the institution, those very features designed to emphasise difference. Staff wanted more conventional names for the academic units—so Social and Industrial Administration became Commerce and Administration. In time, 'schools' became 'faculties'. The interdisciplinary design of degrees was pegged back, as disciplines such as accounting and economics demanded compulsory subjects so their programs could achieve professional accreditation. Programs in law and engineering found their way to campus. With amalgamations, Griffith acquired a number of additional campuses. This required consistency of treatment and parity of esteem for newly acquired colleagues and disciplines from nearby colleges of advanced education. Accreditation requirements diminished opportunities for idiosyncratic course offerings. A more conventional management style emerged to handle increased scale and complexity.

By its twenty-fifth anniversary, Griffith was firmly in the mainstream of Australian universities, with a mission that honoured its origins but reflected contemporary aspirations. As the university's third vice-chancellor,

I was fortunate to lead an institution with strong professional schools and impressive research. I contributed
to standardisation by launching degrees in medicine
and dentistry. Professional programs enabled Griffith
to build a viable local student base across the corridor
from Brisbane to the Gold Coast, and attract large international cohorts. Pioneering original degrees in Asian
Studies and Environmental Science survived, but most
students looked to professional qualifications when
enrolling.

Such changes were perhaps inevitable. A university is
a community, so the choices of students and staff should
influence institutional choices. Still, it is hard not to recall
the frustration of the original Griffith visionaries as they
watched their innovations in pedagogy and governance
quietly replaced by more orthodox practices. These pioneers experienced something familiar from other third-
wave universities: the hold of the Australian idea of a
university over the academic imagination. Griffith rightly
celebrates a distinctive history. Yet differences with its
nearby competitors have diminished over time, as Griffith
has become one institution among many similar players
in a national tertiary system.

The second and third waves of universities in
Australia followed a similar cycle—a desire by policy
makers to increase structural and pedagogical diversity,
brave opening gambits, then a slow but steady move
over decades to a more conventional configuration.
While educational innovators sought to shake the
tradition, the drift from the periphery to the centre
mirrored the aspirations of staff, the financial reality of
attracting students, the practical benefit of a tried and

tested curriculum and a navigable (because familiar) organisational structure.

In John Dawkins, the Minister for Education from 1987 to 1991, Australia would find a politician who would not only embrace the standard model, but write it into law.

4

A UNIFIED NATIONAL SYSTEM

Hannie Rayson's play *Life After George*, published in 2000, was written in the aftermath of great change to higher education in Australia. With an acute eye, Rayson captures tension on campus as an activist government demands economic relevance from universities. The ageing academic George is not convinced by the new agenda. For him the despised reforms are driven by management clones and business paradigms. The university has lost sight of its mission—to produce 'educated citizens. Not just compliant employees'.

Others see the world differently. The irascible George declares:

Your customer-oriented marketing posture means that the least intellectually challenging course is privileged every time. It doesn't make sense to ask

a first-year if we should be teaching postcolonial
history because she doesn't know what it is yet.
She's not yet in possession of the knowledge to
make that decision. But you're obsessed with
pandering to her demands.

His second wife (and fellow academic) responds calmly:

Her demands are fairly straightforward, George.
She wants a job at the end of it.[1]

In one intense period of disruption, beginning in 1987,
such arguments seethed at universities across Australia.
At the time, it seemed the end of everything familiar.
Only with the benefit of distance does it become clear
that bold change in fact reinforced an existing model of
the university, and spread it still further across the nation.

To continue, path dependency requires strong
reinforcement: benefits from travelling down a single
line, constraints to discourage deviation. Expectations
matter—these are nourished by the model that Australians
carry in their minds—but so too does public policy,
as it sets up rules and incentives to shape institutional
behaviour.

Australian universities were established and funded by
colonial and then state governments. The Commonwealth
began paying close attention to the sector during post-
war reconstruction, and established its own national
university in 1946. Three years later, Canberra agreed
to introduce Commonwealth scholarships, seeking more
graduates in the national interest.[2] Within a generation,
Canberra was entirely responsible for funding the sector.
With a sole funder, a single set of rules pushed institutions

towards conformity. The template legislated by John Dawkins remains the purest expression of the Australian tertiary tradition—conservative in design, radical in imposing a standard template across the continent. The Dawkins unified national system is no historical curio but a key force still in the shaping of Australian tertiary institutions and how they are understood.

BEYOND THE BORDERS

To set the scene for national policy change, the story must begin outside the university sector. For while diversity did not take among universities, it could be found in many other post-school education institutions. From the nineteenth century, Australia supported an array of technical and further education colleges, institutes, colleges of divinity, art schools and conservatoria in fields such as nursing, teaching, agriculture and the arts. This lively sector ranged from small colleges with just a few hundred students to large institutes of technology in capital cities. Ownership and governance were equally diverse, running the gamut from autonomous institutions to units within state education departments. Here was the variety of missions and forms not found among universities.

This plurality reflected different histories and purposes. In the university sector, governmental and community expectations weighed heavily on a small number of institutions, each obliged to be all things to all people in their state. In contrast, the non-university higher education sector could occupy many niches. Without research as a primary requirement, the post-school sector employed a diverse array of teachers, including many who combined professional practice with instruction. Artists and writers taught students such as painter

Margaret Preston and the novelist Joan Lindsay, both of whom attended the National Gallery of Victoria Art School. Margaret Olley spent time at Brisbane Central Technical College before transferring to East Sydney Technical College, where fellow painter Charles Blackman also took classes.

Alongside these institutions, many with a history reaching back to the nineteenth century, were colleges of advanced education. Faced with the problem of funding sufficient new university places, the Menzies Government invented this additional category of institution; some were newly created, others based on existing teacher colleges. This catered to changes in the training of professions such as teaching and nursing, and called into being tertiary institutions that looked like universities but cost a good deal less because they did not support research.

The creation of colleges of advanced education reflected concern about expanding the university sector. As Prime Minister Menzies told federal parliament:

> unless there is early and substantial modification of the university pattern, away from the traditional nineteenth-century model on which it is now based, it may not—and I say it with reluctance— be practicable for Australian governments to meet all the needs for university education in Australia and at the same time to achieve the best use of resources in the national interest.[3]

In his influential 1964 report, Sir Leslie Martin, first chairman of the Australian Universities Commission, endorsed non-university institutions as a timely form of specialisation. For Canberra, the distinction between expensive university education and more economical technical training offered a compelling financial rationale. Hence, the Commonwealth embraced a 'binary divide'— research-focused universities on one side of the ledger, and a growing non-university sector on the other. Funds from Canberra would be directed to the college sector. In 1968, university students outnumbered college of advanced education students two to one. A decade later, enrolments were almost equal.

Overall, the system provided students with three post-school education options. They could access technical and further education (TAFE) colleges, funded by the states, with a traditional focus on employment skills and apprenticeship training. Alternatively, an aspiring student could look to colleges of advanced education, many with specialist courses in education and health. Finally, a student could seek professional training in an existing university. In 1972, Peter Karmel, then heading the Australian Universities Commission, optimistically described this higher education landscape as a 'continuum of educational opportunities'. Others used the language of complementary systems.

However, this spectrum of choice proved unstable and short-lived. Institutes and colleges chafed at the status difference implied by a binary divide. They too aspired to offer higher degrees and undertake research. Continuing differences in prestige rankled. Research remained the domain of universities, and this became a point of contention for institute and college of advanced education staff. The dominant model of the university, combining research and teaching, was more attractive than the possibility of creating distinctly different institutions around teaching.

Barely ten years into the formal binary system, mergers began among small institutions in the interests of economy. In 1975, the Victorian Government agreed to combine the Gordon Institute of Technology and the Geelong Teachers' College as Deakin University. This was followed by mergers between universities and colleges in Townsville during 1981 and Wollongong in 1982. In 1986, the Western Australian Institute of Technology further challenged the binary system, negotiating with the state government to become Curtin University.

When John Dawkins, Commonwealth Minister for Employment, Education and Training from 1987 to 1991, came to review higher education policy, the binary divide was already under sustained challenge. At first, the new minister seemed cautious about abandoning the dual-track system. His original 1987 Green Paper suggested the binary divide 'not be set aside lightly', but acknowledged that differences between institutions had 'blurred'. The minister understood the two-sector model had created stratification and jealousy.

Minister Dawkins wanted to expand student access to the system, and sympathised with institute and college claims for university status. His challenge lay in working out how to pay for system expansion. The minister's answer would end institutional diversity and take the process of standardisation to its logical conclusion, imposing a single institutional form on all Australian universities.

THE DAWKINS MOMENT

Minister Dawkins understood the power of policy to remake a system. The ministerial title he adopted—placing 'education' after 'employment'—underlined that university reform would focus on human capital, with explicit economic objectives. Higher education, he argued, must be 'more responsive to the needs of industry, more flexible, more consistent with "national interests and objectives"'.[4] By the time Dawkins left the portfolio in December 1991 to become treasurer, it was a much altered higher education landscape.[5]

Simon Marginson, Professor of International Higher Education at the Institute of Education, University College London, offered a bracing assessment of ministerial craft:

> What Dawkins did was strengthen the normalisation process by systematising the norm of the Australian idea, using the powerful device of competitive emulation to entrench it, while at the same time stepping away from, and/or actively preventing, all forms of state sanctioned diversity of mission and approach, whether binary sector, disciplinary specialist institution, or sanctioned experimentalism.[6]

The new minister listened carefully to concerns from institutes and colleges about their status. Such arguments could be yoked to the minister's aspiration to expand enrolments. By abolishing the binary divide, and extending university status to a wider array of institutions, the minister would double university places. National protocols would define a university and regulate its operations, creating what the minister called a 'unified national system' of higher education.

The Dawkins reforms adopted the familiar template of an Australian metropolitan university and compelled all institutions to conform. The loss of small specialist colleges accentuated similarities. Henceforth, Australian higher education would operate with a single set of funding rates and a preference for three-year undergraduate degrees, using the programs, titles, nomenclature and operating procedures of the nation's founding institutions.

The unified national system accepted only one idea of a university and made it the national standard. The raft of new universities that emerged from the Dawkins reforms were designed in this single image, each a public self-governing institution established through legislation, strongly tipped towards educating the professions, meritocratic, non-residential and comprehensive, with a mission that required teaching and research. They joined existing players already shaped by the Australian tradition.

To fund these changes, the minister ended a fifteen-year experiment with free tertiary education. Undergraduates would now pay fees once earning a salary through a Higher Education Contribution Scheme (HECS). The minister had already allowed universities to charge up-front fees to international students. In time, this would create a huge export industry for Australia, and allow government to reduce financial support for universities.

Minister Dawkins stressed efficiency, and imposed a new minimum size requirement. The Commonwealth would support only research institutions with at least 8,000 full-time students. This meant an end to the independent art schools and music conservatoria, along with the rural and fashion colleges surviving on the periphery of tertiary education. Their demise ended the distinctive educational experience possible only in a small and specialised institution.[7] Some became part of the TAFE sector, but those aspiring to university status faced a difficult decision. Twenty-one institutions failed to meet the size threshold. Their arguments for continued independence were rejected, and so small specialised teaching colleges were absorbed into larger institutions. In the process, Australia lost a diverse set of institutions, even as it gained new universities.[8]

The Dawkins policy prompted a fourth, and largest ever, wave of university foundations. Former teachers' colleges, institutes and colleges of advanced education banded together as new universities in Ballarat, Bathurst, Coffs Harbour and Toowoomba. Some agonised over possibilities before settling into their ultimate shape. The South Australian Institute of Technology and the South Australian College of Advanced Education explored mergers with both Adelaide and Flinders before banding together as the new University of South Australia.[9]

Each amalgamation required a state or territory government to pass enabling legislation, following extensive negotiations among players joining together as a new university. In 1988, just as the Dawkins changes began, the University of Technology, Sydney was established.[10] It was followed the next year by Charles Sturt University, the Northern Territory University, Queensland University of Technology and Western Sydney University. In 1991, Edith Cowan University and the University of South Australia began, while 1992 saw formal commencement of Central Queensland University, RMIT University and Swinburne University. Two years later, the sector welcomed the University of Ballarat (now Federation). Southern Cross University also joined in 1994 after a difficult divorce from the University of New England.

New universities based on former institutes of technology began with strong cultures and seasoned leadership keen to seize new opportunities. Universities emerging from complex amalgamations across colleges were not always so fortunate. Some faced years of internal power struggle in the search for coherence. Deals done in haste were repented at leisure; several universities would spend decades seeking to offload unviable campuses acquired in the heat of change, navigating difficult terrain between communities determined to keep their local university and governing boards concerned about financial viability.

Once Minister Dawkins made mergers necessary for smaller institutions, vice-chancellors scrambled to acquire real estate. One astonished registrar described the operating principles at work as 'greed, and the existence, even in the groves of academe, of corporate raiders'.[11] Some state governments imposed geographically coherent solutions on amalgamations while others deferred to local deals. Thus, while the Queensland Government consolidated former colleges into corridor institutions serving the north, west and south of Brisbane, the Victorian Government signalled preferences but did not enforce outcomes. Instead, 'powerful vice-chancellors' conferred with 'the heads of colleges they coveted', and the deals began.[12] As a result, the University of Melbourne sits only a few hundred metres from a campus of Monash, while the outer Melbourne suburb of Bundoora is home to two university campuses with similar facilities. A university based in Geelong has its largest campus in eastern Melbourne.

Amalgamations also imposed change on existing players. The University of Sydney 'incorporated six institutions as its contribution to the creation of the new unified system, increasing its student load by almost a third, although its academic staff increased by only around 20 per cent'.[13] In the judgement of analysts Julia Horne and Stephen Garton, post-amalgamation Sydney was 'very different' from its earlier self, weaker than more nimble competitors.[14]

By the time the Dawkins wave of mergers concluded, seventy-three higher education providers had become thirty-eight universities. Only three small institutions survived into the following decade: the Australian Maritime College, the Victorian College of the Arts (VCA) and the Batchelor Institute of Indigenous Education. Eventually, the Maritime College would become an institute within the University of Tasmania; the VCA would become a faculty of the University of Melbourne. Only Batchelor endured as a dual-sector tertiary provider outside the university-dominated system, the sole survivor of a more variegated tertiary world before Minister Dawkins.

The Dawkins moment offers a vivid display of path dependency at work. It took an existing model of a university, already credible with students and academics, and mandated it as the national norm. The minister then imposed additional rules around funding, accreditation and operations. He even required a standard semester timetable across the sector. Here, in Page's formulation, path dependency arose from financial rewards for staying with the familiar model, self-reinforcement through academic norms, positive feedback from government for working within the uniform national system, and lock-in through regulation.[15]

For Minister Dawkins, an expanded and more rigorously uniform system addressed a political challenge facing the Hawke Government: how to provide more university places as higher education became central to family aspirations. By reducing difference between institutions, Dawkins rapidly expanded enrolments, providing a rebadged university campus and new tertiary places in many communities. He met his economic objective of expanding the national skills base. The Dawkins moment was the point when Australian higher education tipped from elite to mass—when university attendance became the plausible expectation of millions of school students.

To achieve his goal, Dawkins played on academic status. Prestige resided in institutions with a strong research profile. To garner support, the minister leaned on the normative power of the ideal university type by offering the label—and access to competitive research grants—to new players.

This proved a clever way to divide the tertiary sector. The Australian Vice-Chancellors' Committee warned about 'creating universities out of thin air'.[16] Academics at the ANU offered 'strident' opposition to extending the university name and professorial nomenclature.[17] Yet those in institutes and colleges could celebrate their new titles and access to research-funding schemes. In turn, new universities insisted staff undertake doctoral study, thus encouraging a more uniform set of academic qualifications and research experience across the sector.

It still required external command to complete the imposition of a single model. John Dawkins understood the power of public policy to enforce a single model. In 1987, Canberra provided 83 per cent of university revenue and it used this financial leverage to force sweeping restructures across the entire publicly funded sector. Since states and territories had surrendered the field to the Commonwealth, there was nowhere for universities to seek alternative support. This allowed Canberra to impose consistent national standards. A single Australian Qualifications Framework would fix the length, credit points and standing of certificates and degrees. To ensure parity of esteem, Minister Dawkins insisted on equality of treatment across institutions, despite their uneven starting points. The old and venerable would be subject to the same rules as the newly minted. All would undertake research.

This program would be eroded if a clear hierarchy of institutions emerged. Hence, Canberra insisted on setting the price for study. The middle class would not be permitted, as they could with private schools, to invest greater sums in their children's higher education. To this day, ministerial control of fees remains in force, with degree costs consistent across institutions and the nation.

ASSESSING THE CHANGES

Evaluated against the objective of improving access to higher education, the reforms of 1987–91 constituted a significant and sustained success. Minister Dawkins delivered the nation's most rapid expansion of tertiary education, using a fourth wave of foundations to double university enrolments. In the decades since, hundreds of thousands of Australians have accessed courses once available only to a small cohort. University campuses have become a familiar sight in most Australian towns and cities, and overall participation in higher learning has risen sharply. International students are now found in communities across Australia, and are the nation's largest source of skilled migrants. Access initiatives have lifted the number of Indigenous Australians going to university, while women and people of non-English speaking backgrounds continue to achieve rates of participation at or better than parity.

Minister Dawkins was not focused on facilitating diversity within the higher education system. He achieved his primary objective of rapid system expansion at the expense of difference, driving specialist programs into larger institutions. Subjects too expensive to run vanished, along with the workforce of dedicated staff nurtured by colleges to pursue excellence in teaching.

Critics counted the cost. As a 1995 report prepared for the Organisation for Economic Co-operation and Development (OECD) argued:

> the most astounding result of these changes in Australia has been the degree of uniformity of mission which has developed. No sooner had the new universities gained their new titles than they began to copy their older university counterparts. All wanted to enter the research arena; all wanted to enrol doctoral students irrespective of their infrastructure ... all wanted to introduce Law faculties and most did. The fears of commentators who predicted that instead of creating a unified national system we were about to create a uniform national system (or uniform national mediocrity) were realised. The arguments which the college sector had mounted to demonstrate that while it might be different from universities it was certainly superior to them, and all the avowed emphasis on teaching and diversity disappeared.[18]

Alongside the loss of identity among smaller institutions, the Dawkins reforms intensified concerns about a managerial logic. Discussion of the economy of public universities evokes a rich literature, often offering a narrative of decline in traditional university values.[19] How could academic decisions yield to new management imperatives? Donald Horne recalls a letter of abuse following an acrimonious dispute within the Faculty of Arts at UNSW. 'Your conduct sits better with the professional ethics of a bazaar rug-merchant than those of the chair of an academic faculty,' proclaimed an aggrieved academic.[20] Others wondered aloud whether, in the words of nineteenth-century cultural critic Matthew Arnold, the university could continue to offer the 'best which has been thought and said'.[21]

More often, the analysis focused on the consequences of deterioration in public funding, as tuition costs were pushed onto university students.[22] When education was free and universities reliant on public funding, they were public institutions in every sense. Now Australia's public universities had to raise the majority of their income from students, competitive research grants, philanthropy and commercial activity. Though still public in spirit, and expected to be accountable as public agencies, universities would rely more heavily on private income.[23]

Today, these costs are felt most acutely by those who study and work on campus. If classes are more crowded for students, employment is less certain for staff. Around 120,000 people work in Australian universities, typically at good wages by international comparison, but guaranteed employment disappears as tutorial sizes increase. Staff-to-student ratios have declined across the nation.[24] To contain costs and deal with budget fluctuations, universities deploy a large casual workforce—a shrinking 'tenured core' of older scholars supervising a large periphery of younger academics. One study suggests a majority of Australian academics now work on contingent rather than continuing appointments.[25]

The stringency of tight budgets and larger student loads has encouraged commercial approaches within institutions. This poses a risk, in the words of Stefan Collini, that higher education reform will 'turn some first-rate universities into third-rate companies'.[26]

Murdoch Professor of Politics and International Studies, Kanishka Jayasuriya, suggests the state has imprinted on universities its own economic transformation.[27] Institutions face competitive pressures and growing levels of debt and risk. Platonic ideals of the university give way to discussions about competition, capital and skills. Once scholars but now managers, university leaders find themselves in meetings to choose enterprise information systems, set risk ratings and make commercial decisions alongside academic judgements. Older collegial modes of governance jostle with a more corporate approach to management. The university of popular imagination, a space of witty word-play at academic board meetings and languorous afternoon seminars, is lost from view.

The brief but intensive Dawkins moment gave Australia a much larger higher education system, but one less varied, less resourced for each student, more heavily subject to national rules and regulation. Thus, by ministerial fiat, all Australian universities became essentially—and more than ever—the same.

CONVERGENCE

Minister John Dawkins did not invent the Australian idea of a university—that journey began more than a century earlier—but his new rules and funding arrangements reinforced the single Australian path.

In *The Enterprise University*, Simon Marginson and Mark Considine, Dean of the Faculty of Arts at Melbourne, map similarities and differences within a common Australian model. They maintain that universities are shaped by the state, which imposes conformity, but strive still for individuality.[28] History, curriculum, resources, structures and mission vary, but the study suggests universities can be grouped through association, from the original sandstones to the 'gumtree' universities of the 1960s and 1970s, the former institutes of technology, and the new array of city and regional institutions created in the Dawkins moment.[29]

Marginson and Considine observe that each university has 'its own history and geographic location, its social clusters and particular personalities'.[30] They are keen to acknowledge subtle differences, even as they point to powerful pressures for institutional convergence. Regulation imposes a common template and universities, they suggest, are also prone to copying each other. Since innovation on campus cannot be copyrighted, a new subject area or a clever marketing device will be quickly plagiarised. An idea such as work-integrated learning, encouraging students to spend time in industry while studying, may start in just one institution but spread rapidly. If successful, it may become a standard feature of all Australian universities.

This logic suggests a paradoxical conclusion—that competition can lead to conformity rather than real difference. Dutch social scientist Frans van Vught describes this as a 'reputational race' that drives universities towards the same goals.[31] The phenomenon is known as 'isomorphism', a term appropriated from mathematics. It draws on the Greek *isos,* meaning equal, and *morphe*, to shape, and points to the process by which organisations become more alike over time.

As universities are subject to the same policy environment, employ from the same pool of staff, and compete for the same students by providing much the same set of offerings, they learn from each other. New institutions copy the already successful, and so reinforce a standard model. Academics reinforce hierarchies of status, journals and curricula. Over time, the sector converges around very similar profiles and ways of behaving; 'rational actors make their organisations increasingly similar as they try to change them'.[32] In America, this is sometimes described as 'Harvard Envy'.[33]

Isomorphism is a frame to explain why universities adopt similar structures and missions. Mimicry encourages the foundation of yet more law schools and MBA programs in already crowded markets. It sees innovation ripple across the sector, from the names of schools and faculties to industrial agreements governing employment, until any distinct profile is blurred. Even as they wrap themselves in a rhetoric of difference, tertiary institutions are 'courageous imitations'.[34]

Though a path dependency argument begins from a different point, it supports the same conclusion: amid a wide world of possible institutional design, Australian tertiary education has landed in a narrow confine. There are differences, captured in labels and sector groupings, with some institutions stressing graduate education, others their close links to industry or community. There is stratification by prestige, historic resources and ability to attract research income. These are important differences, but overall the Australian idea of a university is marked less by diversity than by similarity, with few outliers amid many expressions of a shared tradition.

POLICY CHOICES

The model expressed in the unified national system continues to exercise a powerful effect on the Australian imagination, shaping the thinking of both sides of politics about higher education. Faced with an ambitious agenda from Minister Dawkins, the Australian Vice-Chancellors' Committee first cautioned against an expanded university sector, then eventually embraced the minister's definition and made it the criterion for entry to the AVCC.[35] The Dawkins model was further entrenched in the year 2000, when state and federal ministers agreed on a protocol for accrediting universities. This required research in at least three broad fields of study, and so made research a legislated requirement of any Australian university.[36]

For a generation, the standard model of an Australian public university has been fixed in regulation. Institutions vary in size but not in purpose or ambition. Locked into a common funding system and Commonwealth regulatory framework, shaped by isomorphism, Australian universities converge.

Though government has changed hands many times in the years since the incumbency of Minister Dawkins, tertiary education policy remains surprisingly static. There have been reviews and failed legislative attempts at system change, but ministerial successors have retained the logic and regulatory mechanisms they inherited. This so surprised the architect of the system that in September 2016 John Dawkins returned to political debate. He criticised the failure of policy makers to embrace more flexibility and competition between universities. It was time, suggested the former minister, for 'fresh thinking' because his 1987 reforms were now 'completely out of date'.[37]

The former politician offered a stark warning for his successors: 'everyone is sitting on their hands while the world has changed around them'. John Dawkins could see the looming challenge from online providers and alternative approaches to tertiary education. He argued that a model developed in an earlier era, to solve a particular problem around student access, had outlived its usefulness. The regulatory framework Dawkins established now stifled the creativity required to meet the challenge from Silicon Valley.

John Dawkins demonstrated that education policy can shape university practice. He defined the Australian university and hastened it down an existing path. His reforms called forth a system of broad similarity and his legacy persists: Australian universities offer, as their defining rationale, a similar range of undergraduate programs, postgraduate education, and research. There are no specialist institutions, no engineering schools without an arts program, no public institution of scale with a discipline-specific mission. Path dependency and the pressures for convergence have all but eradicated the points of differentiation between Australian universities. In an age of regulated assimilation to a standard model, Australian universities have become more alike over time. In a world of global opportunity and flexibility, this makes them vulnerable.

5

WHAT NEXT?

'Rumour has it that a federal education minister once claimed the country had just one university with around 220 campuses.' So noted a recent survey of Australian university profiles.[1] This is exaggeration, yet the joke stings: the model adopted in 1850 has become an idea that shapes practice across the nation. The logic of path dependency encourages a single acceptable model of a university. The past is not a foreign country, but a continuing reality.

The standard Australian idea of the university has delivered remarkable consistency across the nation. From its origins, the Australian university has been metropolitan in outlook, publicly owned and self-governing, with a strong emphasis on training for the professions. It remains meritocratic, commuter, comprehensive and committed to teaching and research. Australia's institutions operate in a society that is interested in outcomes rather than speculation, egalitarian as though difference among institutions is inherently unfair.[2]

Pragmatism may explain the absence of a distinctive Australian debate about the purpose of a university. There has been little sustained controversy or rigorous contestation—as a state-sponsored institution to meet an agreed need for graduates, the Australian university has fitted comfortably into the community. With few fights over recognition or legitimacy, benign indifference has been the greatest threat.

Those founding the first universities extolled the virtues of higher learning without articulating a theory of education. As practical legislators, they designed an institution that drew on British heritage to address local aspirations. Curriculum content was taken for granted or ceded to the first professorial appointments. Politicians worried instead about securing local skills through an institution open to all. Merit entry spoke to new opportunities, in a colony where transportation of convicts was not abolished until the year in which Sydney established its university.

DIVERSITY AS PRUDENCE

Embodied in thirty-nine public universities, the Australian idea of a university provides a significant, and increasing, cohort of students with tertiary education. Theirs, however, is an education of modest choice. Essentially, only one institutional model is on offer, with providers ranked by prestige and age—rather than by a vibrant ensemble of competing visions, each striving to meet a particular set of interests and ambitions.

A path once taken endures so long as the resulting institutions meet social and economic needs. Few doubt the success of the nation's public universities. Despite some brave experiments, there has been no lasting departure from the road chosen.

At times there were alternatives to university education—the institutes and art colleges of the nineteenth century, a strong network of technical and further education colleges at state level, teacher training institutions and, briefly, colleges of advanced education. Such diversity contracted when John Dawkins legislated small specialist institutions out of existence. In the decades since, the expansion of tertiary places has cut even more deeply into technical courses. Once, students attending TAFE outnumbered their university counterparts. This is no longer the case, with a sharp fall in non-university enrolments. There is now a 'serious problem' for vocational education and training across Australia.[3]

This limited set of post-school education choices is less than ideal. Not every student wants to attend a large, comprehensive, metropolitan-style university. A handful of exceptions—private universities such as Bond, and prestigious if rare specialist institutions such as the National Institute of Dramatic Art—show that other approaches are possible, even if they occupy only tiny niches in a huge system.

Not that change is necessarily popular within the sector itself. When Education, Science and Training Minister Julie Bishop encouraged universities to explore greater institutional diversity, only the universities of Melbourne and Western Australia took up her invitation. In 2008, Melbourne traded undergraduate Commonwealth Supported Places for places in professional degrees at postgraduate level.[4] UWA followed in 2012. This rare example of curricular innovation evoked little enthusiasm from colleagues. Melbourne and UWA found themselves locked out of the demand-driven system by subsequent education ministers who characterised difference as a 'special deal'. A desire to level, to flatten, runs deep in regulators and regulated alike.

Yet global change will raise challenges for a largely undifferentiated system. 'It is the business of the future to be dangerous,' as mathematician Alfred Whitehead said.[5] Australian practice assumes that current norms can endure. One day this may not be true. What happens when students pass by public universities, or world players use brand and technology to establish a local audience? A singular model of a public university might prove too narrow an offering in a fiercely competitive world.

Hence it is time to think again about diversity. If disruption is likely, the public system might consider why earlier attempts to expand the range of universities failed. History suggests diversity cannot be mandated, but it can be encouraged, and this seems prudent in a world of creative destruction. The means to achieve successful change require careful debate. Studies show that 'policies of less state control and more autonomy … do not automatically lead to more diversity in the higher education system'.[6] System design matters too, and this requires a partnership between institutions and policy makers.

Philosopher Hannah Arendt once warned about self-obsession among academics. It is 'difficult to take a crisis in education' too seriously, she said, if it is read as 'unconnected with the larger issues of the century'.[7] To date, the threat from Silicon Valley has not lived up to its publicity. The Australian public university has been shielded from the economic disruption experienced in other industries. Even the trade in higher education remains largely one-way—hundreds of thousands of international students spend money at Australian campuses, but relatively few Australian students choose to study offshore.[8]

It may be that Australia remains too small for serious international competition. So far, only a handful of international universities have tested the local market. Establishing an international campus is an expensive gamble; Southeast Asia and the Middle East offer the prospect of more attractive returns from education investment. For an international investor, Australian government regulation remains an inhibition. Accreditation to take students under the university title requires institutions to invest in expensive and unprofitable research.

This success in locking out the world seems unlikely to endure in an era of free trade agreements. The international student market is worth more than $US100 billion a year in English-speaking countries alone. International providers now follow students offshore. The Chinese government has approved the opening of publicly owned Chinese universities in Laos, Malaysia, Thailand and Japan, with further ventures announced for Cardiff and Seattle.[9] One day, Chinese universities may open in Australia to attract outbound Chinese nationals seeking study abroad, and so compete directly with Australian public universities for the international market.

Though few in number, some international universities already operate in Australia. An offshoot of Carnegie Mellon University from Pittsburgh opened in Adelaide in 2006, aided by a subsidy from the South Australian Government. University College London operates a program in collaboration with the University of South Australia. In 2014, former American President Bill

Clinton launched Torrens University, owned by the inter-national for-profit Laureate group, again in Adelaide. New York University has opened a study-abroad centre for its students in The Rocks, Sydney, and Arcadia University a similar facility in St Kilda, Melbourne.

Alongside global players is a local private sector eager to expand into the university space. Australia is home to globally significant education providers such as IDP, Seek and Navitas. Other private education providers have watched public universities create a multi-billion-dollar-a-year export business. They lobby to remove the research requirement on accreditation. In time, new private teach-ing-only institutions may challenge not just public univer-sities but Bond and Notre Dame also, private institutions that embrace the Australian idea of a university.

As competition arrives, the public university sector will no longer escape Arendt's 'larger issues of the cen-tury'. Globalisation will in time significantly affect universities, just as it has transformed other sectors. 'These trends', argues policy scholar and journalist Ben Wildavsky in his *The Great Brain Race*, are 'hugely ben-eficial to the entire world'.[10] Yet he acknowledges that there must be losers, those swept away by competition.

For-profit companies already work the Australian education market. There are few statistics on the number of Australians studying with global online providers, but a 2015 Austrade estimate reports a local market for e-learning worth $5.9 billion a year.[11] This is an attractive prospect for Silicon Valley players such as the 'MOOCs-for-credit' offered by Kadenze or the self-explanatory offering of nopayMBA.com.

The emergence of tertiary offerings outside the public university sector is indicative of student interest in greater choice. Some students want vocationally orientated courses, more flexible delivery, access to faith-based qualifications rather than the liberal education promoted by public institutions. They look to private offerings. Around 170 'higher education providers' are listed on the register held by the Tertiary Education Quality and Standards Agency, most clustered in IT, business and design.[12] Students are attracted to programs focused on a particular area of employment such as those found at the Endeavour College of Natural Health or the Blue Mountains International Hotel Management School.

It seems unlikely a purely market model will displace the public university system entirely. As education analyst Simon Marginson observes, the traditional public character of tertiary education, linked to research, remains dominant in most nations. 'There is commercial tuition only in parts of vocational training and international education.'[13] Even in the United States, home of the private college, the public sector still educates 73 per cent of university students.

Yet competition, at home and from global players, will grow. As choices widen and a single system fragments, it will be dangerous for all Australian public universities to be stretched out in single file along a narrow road to the deep north. A capacity to meet the market matters if the public sector in education is to prosper amid change.

CAN PUBLIC UNIVERSITIES COPE?

Yes. Australia's public universities already operate simultaneously in two economies—one domestic and regulated, the other international and fiercely competitive.

The public university sector has demonstrated already it can flourish in a variety of markets.

For domestic undergraduates, Canberra controls the maximum price universities can charge. Though the Commonwealth contribution may be small—as little as 16 per cent of the cost of a law or business degree—Canberra sets uniform rates across the nation, regardless of quality or facilities. Not surprisingly, therefore, provision in the domestic undergraduate student market remains largely undifferentiated.

This close regulation, and consequent lack of choice, contrasts sharply with the market for international students. In this unregulated space, Australian public universities make decisions about whom to recruit, what to charge, where to operate. The international education market allows Australia's public universities to pursue independent strategies with little guidance from Canberra.

The contrast could not be more stark. Universities are compliant public agents when dealing with the Commonwealth, but deeply entrepreneurial in international markets. The public and the private sit side by side in the same institution. Every public university has learned how to operate in this dual mode.

In a November 1988 speech, Minister John Dawkins joked that the Australian economy might one day ride on the mortar board.[14] Three decades later, income derived from fee-paying international students enrolled in the Australian education sector exceeds $6 billion a year. Australian universities outperform those of most OECD nations in recruiting international students. Australian institutions have become leading exporters of education, accounting for some 12 per cent of onshore international higher education across the English-speaking world. This is a global market share enjoyed by few other Australian industries.

It is a remarkable achievement. Having catered for just a handful of international students on scholarships a generation ago, Australia now welcomes more than half a million students from abroad to schools, vocational education providers and universities. Most pay the full cost of their education, and keep the lights on at every Australian public university. Education has become the nation's largest service export industry, bringing prosperity to town and city. Like the Latin Quarter in Paris, Australian cities boast streets and suburbs dedicated to education, filled with international students enjoying a few years of study and life in a new society. Public universities have created a new industry for the nation, and made their mark as respected competitors in a new global trade.[15]

This market does not stop at the border. Australian universities are pioneers in going offshore, taking their brand to the region. Some thirty-two Australian universities offer programs internationally, predominantly in Malaysia, Singapore, China, Hong Kong and the Middle East. In 1993, the University of Wollongong led the way with a campus in Dubai. RMIT opened a large and successful campus in Hanoi and then Ho Chi Minh City in 2001, later adding a presence in Barcelona. Monash linked with a commercial partner to open a campus, including a new medical school, in Kuala Lumpur. Monash later expanded to Johannesburg and has become one of the world's largest public providers of international education. Swinburne and Curtin operate in Sarawak, on Borneo, and the University of Southern Queensland in a range of Malaysian cities.[16]

Heading offshore is a hedge against domestic down-turn, a recognition that public funding is no longer sufficient to keep Australia's public universities viable. An international presence requires a global strategy, goals that run beyond a single geographic setting. Such engagement encourages new management skills and levels of organisational sophistication.

An offshore campus becomes a place to trial new approaches to education, an opportunity for experimentation. When James Cook University opened in Singapore in 2003 it developed accelerated programs, allowing students to complete in just two years degrees that require three years of study in Townsville or Cairns. RMIT experimented with similar approaches in Vietnam. Public universities bring innovation home, and allow students to move between local and international campuses.

The international market gives Australian universities a shared identity as places that know about, and embrace, Asia. It also tutors Australian universities about commercial risk, since not every program succeeds. Some international campuses prove financial drains, or generate fees that cannot be repatriated. An ambitious $200 million Singapore campus planned by UNSW failed in 2007.[17] Other universities learned, and shifted from owning campuses to sharing research centres and course delivery with local partners in India and China.

The international market has a mixed effect on diversity. It can strengthen uniformity, because international students pay close attention to institutional rankings. As Marginson asserts, the dominance of the research-intensive university in rankings 'bears down hard' on any institution that does not follow this model.[18] Australia's public universities benefit from their heritage as respected research institutions, with an implicit government guarantee of quality. Domestic operations provide a stable platform for international marketing. The need to do well in rankings reinforces a common commitment to research.

On the other hand, when playing internationally each university must make its own offer to the market. While pressures at home encourage homogeneity, abroad the university sector can be more expansive. Universities promote their own region as the best place to study, stress opportunities for internships and promise international students a distinctive local experience. It is great to be an Australian university, but not enough. Potential international students, with a world to explore, must be convinced that a Bachelor of Mechatronic Engineering at Wollongong or a Bachelor of Wine Business from Charles Sturt University is their best choice.

Global education rewards innovation and punishes the slow moving. As Schumpeter cautions, markets destroy and build simultaneously. When students can exercise choice, for better or worse they challenge isomorphism. As they work internationally, Australian public universities test new paths, build new capabilities, learn how to emphasise what is distinctive. They also build unique student bodies, connecting local institutions to Asia and beyond, learning how to operate across the region. Working abroad has prepared Australian higher education for competition at home.

POLICY DESIGN

When the freight train line arrived in Illinois, it left little time for local fruit and vegetable growers to adjust. Their protected market vanished overnight. Like the fisherfolk of Oxford, all they could do was watch as cheaper and better options were delivered by new technology.

The digital revolution in higher education has changed much already on campus, but not yet undermined fatally the fundamentals. Public universities adapt, not least because they work already in Asian markets and understand the need for agility amid the remorseless logic of global scale and capital.

To endure over the longer run, public universities need a new policy conversation. These are public institutions, and government should not just abandon the field; rather, it should think again about the higher education sector's aims and purpose. Australia needs a viable university system, and universities in turn require a policy environment that allows *innovation* and rewards *difference*. We should question the endless line of education ministers who speak about the need for diversity yet tighten regulation further. As one senior observer contended, 'I don't think there is a lot of terribly strategic national-level decisions made about higher education in Australia'.[19] As change looms, now is the time for intelligently designed higher education policy.

Four initiatives could fundamentally change the rules for public universities and their contribution to the nation.

The first requires thinking about post-school education as a single sector—the 'vision thing' conspicuously lacking from discussions of education, which focus almost exclusively on funding arrangements.

To be effective, a national framework must embrace the entirety of post-school education. State and national governments worry, rightly, about the decline in vocational training. Experiments in private provision have produced at times scandalous results. The future of TAFE, apprenticeships and the world of education outside universities will not be resolved until the policy framework deals with all the variables. To encourage open-ended enrolments in university courses, then puzzle over the collapse of other forms of training, is to miss something obvious. As a famous study of mass and elite education systems by Berkeley scholar Martin Trow notes, a viable comprehensive system for a nation requires a combination of institutional types.[20]

A single post-school policy raises questions, notably around federalism. Universities are funded by Canberra, while much trade training belongs to the states. As university student numbers rose from 2012 under the demand-driven system of open enrolments, 'most states began to reduce investment' in vocational education.[21] Yet the challenges of providing Australians with meaningful educational choice will not resolve until all pieces are on the table, ready for a single conversation.

The second potential reform is technical in nature, but important in consequence. The funding regimes for both teaching and research in Australia's public universities pay little attention to the actual cost of either activity. This has a chilling effect on diversity. It requires that universities provide 'profitable' courses to help fund expensive specialist offerings and subsidise research. As a result, no institution can afford to specialise in a discipline such as engineering or the visual arts, because bankruptcy would follow without the cushion of large law, business, nursing and teaching courses to pay the bills.

In a market, universities would develop specialisations and support these by charging the real cost of course delivery. Since Commonwealth regulation prohibits this, it is imperative the course fees authorised by Canberra pay close attention to actual cost. Otherwise, every public university, as at present, must hedge its bets through complex internal cross-subsidies.

The third reform would address the large size and complexion of existing institutions. To quote a Group of Eight pro-vice-chancellor interviewed in the study led by sociologist Bill Lacy:

> The issue has to do with institutional diversity. Since we created the Unified National System, as it used to be called 25 years ago, in a sense, we have a flat system. All of our universities are expected to be research universities. They are typically comprehensive across their disciplines. They all operate by and large under the same policy settings ...
>
> Now, the problem with a flat system for Australia is that it does not offer the diversity that the nation needs. It is also really costly to run because, fundamentally, you have people on teaching-research academic appointments across the whole sector. Many of them are not research-active at all. My argument then is differentiation of the system in Australia is really important. We need teaching-only universities or colleges but it is extraordinarily difficult to imagine how we get to that point because at the moment, to have the title university, you have to be a research institute.[22]

This argues that Australia would benefit from some institutions without a research requirement. In order to encourage wider coverage of skills, opportunity and disciplines, not all universities should be compelled by law to embrace research. An opportunity to focus on teaching and engagement would change fundamentally the economics of at least some public universities.

Of course, no government will (or should) contemplate changing the status of existing institutions. To remove research from an established university would be politically impossible for universities closely linked to their communities. More importantly, it is unnecessary. There is another way. Greater system diversity can be secured by addition, through the creation of new public tertiary institutions.

After the rapid formation of fourth-wave universities in the Dawkins moment, the impetus for new institutions slowed dramatically. The University of the Sunshine Coast was not listed separately for Commonwealth funding until 1999, and in 2003 a merger between the Northern Territory University, the Menzies School of Health Research and Centralian College created Charles Darwin University. Open Universities Australia expanded its online offerings, and a specialist private University of Divinity represented continuing collaboration across a number of theological colleges. Otherwise, the university system has experienced little structural change for some decades.

Meanwhile, a sharp rise in enrolments has been accommodated within existing universities. As a result, Australian public universities have grown to unprecedented size. Monash now welcomes more than 70,000 effective full-time students. Even the smallest public university, Charles Darwin, accommodates around 10,350 higher education and TAFE enrolments. The public sector has no small, intimate alternatives—no liberal arts college with an annual intake of just a few hundred students, no Caltech with only 2,240 students or Princeton with 8,100 enrolments.

In the 1960s and 1970s, Australia created new universities to anticipate and absorb student demand. Since 2001, the tertiary sector has grown by more than 70 per cent. This could have supported fifteen or more additional universities. Instead, all expansion has been absorbed within existing institutions. By inflating established players rather than inventing anew, the higher education system has reinforced existing institutional patterns.

This narrowness of institutional type is found also in the United Kingdom. Economist Alison Wolf laments a 'university only universe'. She recalls that Britain was once home to colleges of advanced technology and thirty or so polytechnics that offered an alternative to full degrees. Polytechnical colleges were established with 'close links to local labour markets' and a stress on part-time study. By 1992, all had converted into universities.

Wolf compares this with the organisational variety that continues in other nations. In 1970, Germany established *Fachhochschulen* as distinctive technical universities:

> Today, they thrive, and are central to the country's engineering excellence. The US has community colleges. Canada has well-resourced tertiary colleges, specialising in vocational diplomas. Or take the Netherlands. The Dutch haven't created a university since 1976. Instead they expanded their respected 'higher professional education' system, taught in *Hogescholen* which are close to the vision once held for polytechnics. By contrast,

since 1976 in the UK, we have created another 89
universities (although a few have since merged),
and not a single major alternative institution.[23]

It is time to consider a fifth wave of public institutions.
This is not a return to a binary divide but a chance to
create new specialist institutions, excellent in a defined
field of knowledge. They could straddle sectors, offering
vocational as well as university qualifications. Diversity
might embrace institutional size, mission, student mix,
course offerings, mode and language of instruction,
undergraduate and postgraduate offerings, generalist
and professional programs.

A commitment to a specific academic discipline is a
way to create identity, develop depth and bind together
an institution. Thus, Australia should welcome a new tertiary institution that makes its principal contribution in
technology or agriculture. There could be industry-spe-
cific institutions attending to aviation, banking or software engineering. Institutional innovation might break
down the current national idea of tertiary education as
necessarily large, comprehensive and research intensive.

An existing approach could be developed more
widely across Australia—universities that also offer TAFE
courses, along with the many TAFE colleges keen to
offer degrees in their areas of expertise. The dual-sector
experiment in Australia deserves more consideration as a
way to encourage traffic across levels of education.

Now is the right time to design and launch new public
players, and so expand the curricula on offer. Alongside
more choice for Australian students, a rich ecosystem of
institutional types would enhance Australia's international appeal as a study destination.

Integrated as a single reform agenda, these three proposals could transform higher education: a single policy perspective over the post-school sector, funding for teaching and research that reflects actual costs, and the creation of new universities to accommodate growth. Implemented, they would allow greater diversity, give students more choice and provide some insurance against disruption of the established model.

There is a fourth possible policy intervention, but it is contentious and likely to be unpopular within the sector. Higher education in the United States runs without national supervision, relying on state-based accreditation and federal laws governing access to student grants. In the United Kingdom, governments experiment with agencies designed to oversee institutional finances, learning outcomes and research, while emphasising institutional autonomy.

By contrast, governments in Asia plan for the tertiary education system. In Singapore, the ministry takes institutional mission seriously, insisting each university and institute pursue vigorously its legislated mandate rather than converge on a single, familiar model. In Hong Kong, the University Grants Committee (UGC) must ensure stability of policy and equality of treatment for public universities.[24] The UGC holds universities to their stated missions when allocating capital and agreeing to new course offerings.

Over many decades, UGC staff have developed detailed knowledge about universities in Hong Kong, and so create institutional memory about policy logic. This intellectual capital encourages reflection on lessons learned and thoughtful consideration of future prospects. Through careful planning, Hong Kong has achieved system differentiation unknown in Australia, covering a wide spectrum from the small liberal-arts-focused Lingnan University, with just 3,000 students, to the large, research-intensive and highly ranked Hong Kong University.

If Australia is to create a more diverse system, it needs similar commitment to system design. Simply creating new institutions is not sufficient, as the many failed attempts at difference make clear. The moment requires clear-eyed assessment by policy makers to understand why previous attempts to create diversity did not deliver, and a common vision and policy stability to allow future institutional exploration and change.

A revived Australian Tertiary Education Commission is one mechanism that would enable sector-wide review, analysis and action on lessons learned. The name reflects coverage of the whole field, with legislated authority to deal with local jealousies. A representative board is essential, to address differences in sectors, focus and geography. A new regulatory body could oversee policy implementation from vocational education to doctoral programs, and so provide Australia with a coherent framework for higher education.

This Australian Tertiary Education Commission would be the guardian of intelligent policy design, leaving ministers to set overall direction for the sector through legislation without involvement in day-to-day adminis-tration. A commission cannot impose diversity, but a sec-tor-wide policy perspective, reform of funding rates and research support, and nurturing of new players would encourage difference.

It may seem counterintuitive to recommend an expert oversight body in the midst of an accelerating, rapacious and innovative set of challenges to public universities. Institutions would not welcome another regulatory agency. Yet the practice of regulation has changed greatly in recent decades. New agencies overseeing industries such as superannuation and business registration use their mandated authority to enforce transparent operating rules. They 'hold the ring', ensuring a space for experimentation and competition. Universities can make investment choices with some confidence that the next minister for higher education will not cut funding and move on, leaving chaos in their wake.

British research policy operates on the Haldane Principle, an agreement that qualified researchers rather than politicians should make decisions about where public research money is spent. As a result, universities do not lobby ministers seeking special deals for research investment but must argue their case to a panel of experts. Reasons are published with decisions.

The Haldane Principle could be applied more widely to university policy by empowering an Australian Tertiary Education Commission to set relative funding rates within an overall budget set by government. An independent commission charged with exclusive authority to distribute all public funding for tertiary education according to transparent operating procedures would stop universities behaving like mendicants, always hassling government for some local advantage.

As sector analysts Peter Coaldrake and Lawrence Stedman argue:

> Rather than categorising institutions into neat boxes or rewarding or penalising institutions with simplistic measures, we need to allow the

> emergence of different ways of adapting the university ideal to meet society's changing needs within the resources society provides, whether these be public or private, campus-based or online, research intensive or otherwise.[25]

By providing policy stability, a commission could help a more diverse sector to emerge.

THE FUTURE

The premise of this essay is that even successful industries face disruption—by a new train line that brings distant produce to Chicago or internet advertising that destroys the business model of newspapers. A venerable history does not confer immunity. The logic of encouraging diversity therefore speaks not just to greater student choice or more specialist institutions able to invest in depth rather than breadth. The goal, fundamentally, is to ensure public institutions can adapt as the environment alters.

Diversity is easy to praise, difficult to achieve. As historian of universities Robert Anderson argues, a pluralist higher education system requires 'more open acceptance that universities have different missions, interpreting the idea of the university in different ways'. We must recognise that 'embracing differentiation is healthier than denying it'.[26]

Official reports have long despaired over the uniformity of the Australian higher education system. When the West Review reported to the Howard Government in 1998, it could see only a narrow band of institutions:

> Apart from differences in emphasis ... Australian public universities are all comprehensive

institutions of higher education. The current system of centralised resource allocation and controls over tuition fees encourages 'a one size fits all' system. While there is some diversity in mission, clientele, mode of delivery, educational philosophy and style within the system, far greater differentiation is possible and, indeed, desirable.[27]

Habit is a lane cut deep into the landscape. It provides a way to make quick and safe choices. Design choices from the middle of the nineteenth century have endured, in part because universities did their job well, in part because the direction of travel was reinforced over a century and a half of student expectations, academic culture and policy choices. Path dependency is part habit, part staying with what works, part self-imposed strategy. The original idea has proved compelling, defeating even legislated instructions to be different.

Though technology looms, public universities do not face inevitable ruin. They continue to compete despite complications caused by their size and complexity. With policy reform, universities can be even more responsive, finding their own niches in a growing industry. Though previous attempts at diversification did not bear enduring results, circumstances on the ground demand that we try again.

Not every university will feel a need to change. A strong market endures in the United States for research-led universities with a vibrant campus life. There will always be students in Australia who value the chance to interact with active scholars, ruminate over the summer while travelling or working, spend time in a laboratory or on a research project. Former University of Adelaide

Vice-Chancellor Warren Bebbington predicts successful institutions will include universities that articulate their 'traditional mission powerfully', stay 'true to their core values and teaching modes' and project a 'powerful connection with their geographic place'.[28]

Yet continued expansion of the status quo is an expensive option. Even if existing universities can maintain their current character, further growth using the standard model may not deliver what the nation or its students need.

Reflecting on the purpose of a university education, academic Alice Garner suggests what great institutions 'teach us is how to ask hard questions, where to look for other people's answers, and if none is satisfactory, how to go about coming up with our own'.[29]

Asking hard questions and chancing answers is not just an educational goal but good advice for the sector. Public universities face disruption knowing other industries have braved the difficult transition from protected local provision to global participation. To encourage adaptation to global markets, governments abandon close controls and adopt, instead, a 'hands-off' regulatory framework that stresses fair competition, minimum acceptable service standards, and transparency. Unprofitable public providers are allowed to fold. The sector that emerges from exposure to international competition looks very different from its earlier self, which operated in the days of isolation and uniformity.

Canberra is yet to contemplate such a transition for higher education, though Australian public universities have demonstrated their ability to compete internationally. As the higher education sector becomes more international, with services traded in both directions, the familiar Australian idea of the public university may prove too constricting. Stately progression along a familiar road can halt abruptly. So now is the time to look for answers, and invent new ones if none is found satisfactory.

There is still time for local choices. A new policy framework could think about post-school education as a single system. 'Diversity will not be achieved if there is a perception that non-traditional universities are inferior', observes educational consultant and scholar Vin Massaro.[30] Universities, colleges, TAFEs and online providers all have much to share with students, and it should be possible for consumers to move seamlessly through the different modes of institution. The divide among sectors hinders clarity in policy thinking. A single-system approach would provide pathways from vocational to tertiary education, with one set of rules to accredit institutions, assure quality and fund students.

The aim of intelligent policy design is not to force change, since none of us can predict the future, but to encourage greater experimentation and adaptation. We need many different Australian ideas of a university, not just variations on a single theme.

The sector is ready for change, and needs a reform agenda to match. Otherwise, markets may annihilate existing players. Schumpeter recorded how quickly new technologies removed a local economy around Chicago. Marx evoked the pitiless march of markets, working relentlessly without respect for tradition. A long pedigree and fine stone buildings offer little defence against the restless inventiveness of entrepreneurs, who see opportunities to remake the higher education model conceived in Australia in 1850.

To date, the story of universities in Australia is the steady expansion of a single model, punctuated by occasional attempts to break away from the shared path. The result is a system characterised more by similarity than diversity. The original metropolitan model remains the aspiration of most students and staff, a practical solution to providing higher education rather than the expression of an abstraction.

The Australian idea of a university has been the still point in a turning world, a constant in national life. Yet paths eventually come to an end. They arrive at their destination or fall into disrepair as new roads provide better alternatives. Fortunately we have a public university sector skilled at responding to profound challenge. With the right policy settings, Australia can trade a single history for diversity, one path for many. If we understand history, we need not be its victims.

ACKNOWLEDGEMENTS

This small essay has prosaic origins: a curiosity about the uniformity of Australian higher education when confronted with the diversity of American experience. As a post-doctoral fellow in Cambridge, Massachusetts, comparing the technical brilliance of MIT with the intellectual ambitions of Harvard, I wondered why Australia lacked such dramatic contrasts. Scale and wealth mattered, but there seemed more at work.

From this modest inquiry more strands followed: the interplay of history and policy, regulatory choices and budgetary realities, the unexamined cultural norms that encourage Australians towards a single, narrow path for tertiary education.

It is a subject touched in passing in several essays for the *Griffith Review* and the *Australian Book Review* before a 2013 exchange with University of Melbourne colleague Professor Rai Gaita. Over lunch, emails and eventually articles in *Meanjin*, Rai and I talked about the Australian experience of higher education. Though our conclusions spoke to different concerns, the exchange proved stimulating and provocative, a conversation never quite finished but now explored further in this book. I remain grateful to Rai for the invitation to think about the subject.

I learned much also while working with Chief Investigator Stuart Macintyre, and Gwilym Croucher, Julia Horne and Stephen Garton on a 2015 Australian Research Council project examining the history and impact of Minister John Dawkins on higher education. The seminars, lunchtime conversations and publications from the project, and the immense archive of materials collected by the team, deepened significantly a shared understanding of the Dawkins moment.

This essay has a specific and limited focus: the form and mission of public universities. It provides a chance to expand on brief remarks about organisation in *The Republic of Learning*, my 2010 Boyer Lectures. Much remains to say about private institutions and vocational education, but others are more expert in these topics.

These pages are finished as I close a long and enjoyable tenure as vice-chancellor at the University of Melbourne, but do not (I hope) offer autobiography disguised as policy analysis. I avoid more than passing reference to developments at Melbourne and only one section draws directly on personal experience. This is a discussion in Chapter 4 of changes at Griffith University, my academic home for nearly twenty years.

My thanks to Louise Adler from Melbourne University Publishing for commissioning the volume and to MUP Executive Publisher Sally Heath and her team for steering it through to publication. I am indebted to Julianne Schultz and Peter Rose for the earlier commissions to write on the topic (for how can I know what I think until I try to write it down?).

A number of colleagues have been generous in reading the essay in draft and offering detailed comments. My thanks to Sharon Bell, Mark Considine, Gwilym

Croucher, Carolyn Evans, Julia Horne, Gregor Kennedy, Stuart Macintyre, Peter McPhee, Simon Marginson, Ian Marshman, Vin Massaro, Andrew Norton and Carolyn Rasmussen. Each has asked challenging questions, corrected errors and suggested new lines of thought. I am awed by their knowledge of higher education policy.

Above all, I have worked closely on this book with University of Melbourne colleague David Threlfall. His pursuit of additional material, editorial suggestions on drafts, engagement with the mechanics of publication and keen eye for the telling anecdote have made this journey a pleasure. Katia Ariel provided provocative questions and expert editing.

Finally, my thanks to Margaret Gardner for her comments on the manuscript and a conversation about universities through our lives together.

Melbourne
August 2017

NOTES

Prologue

1   Lacy et al., *Australian Universities at a Crossroads: Insights from Their Leaders and Implications for the Future*, 2017, p. 52.

2   Personal communication from Sharon Bell, 2017.

3   Newman, *The Idea of a University Defined and Illustrated: In Nine Discourses Delivered to the Catholics of Dublin*, 1996 (f.p. 1852); an introduction to Jill Ker Conway's influence on Smith College is available through the college's historical encyclopedia: see Smithipedia, 'President Jill Ker Conway', 2017; Wilson, *Princeton in the Nation's Service*, 21 October 1896; Kerr, *The Uses of the University*, 2001.

4   Horne, *Into the Open: Memoirs 1958–1999*, 2000, p. 216.

5   Walsh, *Lapsing*, 1986, p. 251.

6   Collins, 'Political Ideology in Australia: The Distinctiveness of a Benthamite Society', *Daedalus*, 1985.

7   Collini, *What Are Universities for?*, 2012, pp. 24–5.

8   Leckart, 'The Stanford Education Experiment Could Change Higher Learning Forever', *Wired*, 20 March 2012.

1   End of the line?

1   In Ignatieff, *Isaiah Berlin: A Life*, 1998, p. 225.

2   Backus, 'Commentary: Creative Destruction Meets Higher Education', *The Washington Post*, 19 May 2013.

3   *The Economist*, 'Higher Education: Creative Destruction', 28 June 2014.

4   Kao, *Innovation Nation*, 2007, p. 264.

5   Schumpeter, *Capitalism, Socialism and Democracy*, 1975 (f.p. 1942), pp. 82–6.

6   Schumpeter, *The Economics and Sociology of Capitalism*,
    1991, p. 349; Schumpeter, *Capitalism, Socialism and
    Democracy*, p. 84.
7   Woolley, 'The Coming of the Railway to Oxford', *South
    Oxford Community Centre*, 2016; Woolley, 'How the
    Railway Changed Oxford', *Oxfordshire Local History
    Association Journal*, 2013–14, p. 31.
8   A quote attributed to Rector of Lincoln College Mark
    Pattison, in Stoppard, *The Invention of Love*, 1998, p. 17.
9   In Thomas, 'The Chase', *London Review of Books*,
    20 October 2016, p. 15.
10 This description of Rutgers and the University of Phoenix
    draws on Davis, 'The Rising Phoenix of Competition:
    What Future for Australia's Public Universities?', *Griffith
    Review*, 2006.
11 Rosen, *Change.edu: Rebooting for the New Talent
    Economy*, 2011, p. 150.
12 Trowbridge, 'University of Phoenix Parent Accepts Federal
    Amendments for Buyout Approval', *Phoenix Business
    Journal*, 21 December 2016.
13 Newman offered an earlier version of this argument,
    discounting even books when compared with personal
    conversation: 'no book can convey the special spirit and
    delicate peculiarities of its subject with that rapidity and
    certainty which attend on the sympathy of mind with mind,
    through the eyes, the look, the accent, and the manner,
    in casual expressions thrown off at the moment, and
    the unstudied turns of familiar conversation'. Newman,
    Historical Sketches, vol. 3, 1889, pp. 8–9.
14 An insight that Stuart Macintyre attributes to historian
    and Vice-Chancellor Alan Gilbert, himself a pioneer in
    online learning.
15 Leckart, 'The Stanford Education Experiment Could
    Change Higher Learning Forever', *Wired*, 20 March 2012.
16 Udacity, 'About Us', 2017.
17 Based on a visit to Udacity in January 2016.
18 In Leckart, 'The Stanford Education Experiment Could
    Change Higher Learning Forever'.
19 Wood, 'The Future of College?', *The Atlantic*, September
    2014.

20 Ibid.
21 *The Economist*, 'Established Education Providers v New
    Contenders: Alternative Providers of Education Must Solve
    the Problems of Cost and Credentials', Special report,
    12 January 2017.
22 For a characteristic example, see Toren, 'Top 100
    Entrepreneurs Who Made Millions without a College
    Degree', *Business Insider Australia*, 20 January 2011.
23 Cohan, 'Why Peter Thiel Is Wrong to Pay Students to
    Drop Out', *Forbes*, 15 June 2011. Cohan's piece refers to a
    paper by Lange et al., 'Human Assets and Entrepreneurial
    Performance: A Study of Companies Started by
    Business School Graduates', *Journal of Business and
    Entrepreneurship*, 2012.
24 The list is drawn from Dodd, 'New Study Reveals $40
    Billion Is Invested in Education Technology', *Australian
    Financial Review*, 8 May 2017, p. 12.
25 *The Economist*, 'Higher Education: Creative Destruction'.
26 Schumpeter, *Capitalism, Socialism and Democracy*, p.
    83 note 2; Eldredge and Gould, 'Punctuated Equilibria:
    An Alternative to Phyletic Gradualism', in Schopf (ed.),
    Models in Paleobiology, 1972.
27 Fain, 'Fine Print and Tough Questions for the Purdue–
    Kaplan Deal', *Inside Higher Ed*, 30 May 2017.
28 Rosen, *Change.edu*, pp. 181–93.

2   The metropolitan university

1   This chapter draws on Davis, 'The Australian Idea of a
    University', *Meanjin*, 2013.
2   Thrift, 'The University of Life', *New Literary History*,
    2016, p. 402.
3   It is a truth universally acknowledged in jeremiads on
    universities that managers have multiplied on campus while
    academic recruitment languishes. It is a surprise therefore
    to note that a systematic American study, with data from
    1987 to 2013, finds that the 'share of college employees
    who are executives, administrators, or managers has not
    changed appreciably over time'. See Hinrichs, *Trends in
    Employment at US Colleges and Universities, 1987–2013*,
    2016.

4   Carnegie Classification of Institutions of Higher Education,
     'Basic Classification Description', 2017.
5   Campion College in Sydney, a private institution, would
     be classified as a 'baccalaureate college: arts & science
     focus' in the Carnegie schema. The private University of
     Divinity would likely be called a 'special focus institution',
     though the Carnegie classification has little to say about
     theological schools. Dual-sector institutions offer both
     vocational and bachelor qualifications. Category R
     in the Carnegie classification offers three variants—
     highest, *higher* and *moderate* research activity, with
     some distinctions between universities with medical
     and veterinary schools and those without, so Australian
     universities spread across these sub-categories.
6   Matchett, 'Uni Lobby Laments: We're Being Punished for
     Peak Performance', *Campus Morning Mail*, 4 May 2017.
7   Stinchcombe, *Constructing Social Theories*, 1968, in
     Schwartz, 'Down the Wrong Path: Path Dependence,
     Increasing Returns, and Historical Institutionalism', 2004.
8   Pierson, *Politics in Time: History, Institutions, and Social
     Analysis*, 2004.
9   David, 'Clio and the Economics of QWERTY', *The
     American Economic Review*, 1985. See also Anderson,
     'Why is QWERTY on Our Keyboards?', *BBC Culture*,
     13 December 2016.
10   Liebowitz and Margolis, 'The Fable of the Keys', in
     Spulber (ed.), *Famous Fables of Economics*, 2002.
11   Pierson, 'The New Politics of the Welfare State', *World
     Politics*, 1996, p. 175.
12   Page, 'Path Dependence', *Quarterly Journal of Political
     Science*, 2006, p. 87.
13   Schwartz, 'Down the Wrong Path: Path Dependence,
     Increasing Returns, and Historical Institutionalism', p. 5.
14   Page, 'Path Dependence', p. 88.
15   Pietsch, Em*pire of Scholars: Universities, Networks and the
     British Academic World, 1850–1939*, 2013, p. 5.
16   Alan Atkinson suggests that the University of Toronto, as
     with Sydney, was influenced by Anglican thought, with
     concessions to secularism in the founding constitution a
     nod to divergent protestant beliefs within a nation assumed

fundamentally to be Christian. Atkinson, '"Do Unto
Others": Australia and the Anglican Conscience, 1840–56
and Afterwards', in Macintyre, Layman and Gregory (eds),
A Historian for All Seasons: Essays for Geoffrey Bolton,
2017.

17 Turney, Bygott and Chippendale, *Australia's First:
A History of the University of Sydney, Vol. 1: 1850–1939*,
1991, pp. 7–8.

18 Longo, 'History Honours, 1901–2010', in Prest (ed.), *Pasts
Present: History at Australia's Third University*, 2014,
p. 116.

19 McCord and Purdue, *British History 1815–1914*, 2007,
p. 376.

20 From the 1963 Robbins Report, in Collini, 'From Robbins
to McKinsey', *London Review of Books*, 25 August 2011.

21 In *Eminent Victorians*, published in 1918, Lytton Strachey
provides a sympathetic picture of Newman's failure,
blaming not the concept but local clerical politics and 'the
inertia of the Irish authorities'.

22 Collini, *What Are Universities for?*, 2012, p. 195.

23 Mill, 'Inaugural Address to the University of St Andrews',
in Robson (ed.), *The Collected Works of John Stuart Mill,
Vol. XXI—Essays on Equality, Law, and Education*, 1867.

24 Persse, 'Wentworth, William Charles (1790–1872)',
Australian Dictionary of Biography, 1967.

25 Collini suggests that at least three different kinds of
British universities were operating at the beginning of
the twentieth century: 'the Oxbridge model: residential,
tutorial, character-forming. There was the Scottish/London
model: metropolitan, professorial, meritocratic. And there
was the "civic" model ("Redbrick" was a later coinage):
local, practical, aspirational'. *What Are Universities for?*,
p. 28.

26 Horne and Sherington, '"Dominion Legacies": the Case
of Australia', in Schreuder (ed.), *Universities for a New
World: Making an International Network in Global Higher
Education, 1913–2013*, 2013.

27 Ibid., p. 285.

28 Colony of New South Wales Legislative Council, *Votes and
Proceedings*, Friday 28 June 1850, p. 44.

29 Jayasuriya, 'Transforming the Public University: Market
    Citizenship and Higher Education Regulatory Projects',
    in Thornton (ed.), *Through a Glass Darkly: The Social
    Sciences Look at the Neoliberal University*, 2014, p. 90.
30 In calculating this figure there is a definitional argument
    about whether the Australian Catholic University counts
    as a public institution (it certainly relies on public funding
    and is established by legislation, but takes the form of a
    company). In 2015, the Department of Education and
    Training recorded that private universities make up 1.1 per
    cent of overall teaching load, with TAFE contributing
    a further 0.19 per cent. If ACU is counted as a private
    institution also, the private higher education effort
    rises to 2.8 per cent. In either case, the system remains
    overwhelmingly public.
31 Turney, Bygott and Chippendale, *Australia's First*, pp. 40–1.
32 *University of Sydney Act 1850*, United Kingdom.
33 Serle, *John Monash: A Biography*, 1982, p. 479.
34 A quote from the *Sydney Morning Herald* of 5 October
    1849, cited in Hirst, *Freedom on the Fatal Shore:
    Australia's First Colony*, 2008, p. 216.
35 Though midwifery is identified in the founding statute as
    an essential skill for the colony, women were not allowed
    to sit the matriculation exam until 1871 and not granted
    admission to the university until 1881.
36 Selleck, *The Shop: The University of Melbourne, 1850–
    1939*, 2003, p. 47.
37 Cable, 'Woolley, John (1816–1866)', *Australian Dictionary
    of Biography*, 1976.
38 Calculating exactly what constitutes a professional program
    can be challenging, and this figure is an estimate based on
    close reading of the University of Sydney annual report.
    On this count, graduate courses account for 69.2 per cent
    of current enrolments at the University of Sydney. I am
    grateful for personal communication from Julia Horne in
    2017 clarifying the early pattern of enrolments at Sydney.
39 Horne and Sherington, 'Extending the Educational
    Franchise: The Social Contract of Australia's Public
    Universities, 1850–1890', *Paedagogica Historica*, 2010,
    p. 210.

40 Ibid., p. 211.

41 As Turney, Bygott and Chippendale argue: 'A university
    education, or at least a university degree, was the
    prerogative of those, and only those, who subscribed to the
    established religion'. *Australia's First*, p. 6.

42 Persse, 'Wentworth, William Charles (1790–1872)'. The
    recommendations of the Royal Commission of 1850
    opened the doors of Oxford to non-Anglicans, suggest
    McCord and Purdue, *British History 1815–1914*, p. 376.

43 Horne, 'Political Machinations and Sectarian Intrigue in
    the Making of Sydney University', *Journal of the Australian
    Catholic Historical Society*, 2015, p. 5.

44 Atkinson, '"Do Unto Others"', p. 132.

45 Ibid., pp. 132–3.

46 The visitor was Thomas Donovan in 1915, who would
    later help establish Newman College at Melbourne. In
    Selleck, *The Shop*, p. 574.

47 Colony of New South Wales Legislative Council, *An Act
    to Incorporate and Endow the University of Sydney*, 1
    October 1850; Horne and Sherington, *Sydney: The Making
    of a Public University*, 2012, p. 7: 'The foundation of the
    University of Sydney as a secular and non-denominational
    institution was integral to its character as a public
    institution'.

48 Horne and Sherington, 'Extending the Educational
    Franchise'.

49 Cable, Turney and Bygott, *Australia's First: A Pictorial
    History of the University of Sydney 1850–1990*, 1994,
    p. 12.

50 Selleck, *The Shop*, p. 132, on the origins of Trinity College,
    the first at the University of Melbourne.

51 Turney, Bygott and Chippendale, *Australia's First*, p. 137.

52 Linn, *The Spirit of Knowledge: A Social History of the
    University of Adelaide North Terrace Campus*, 2011, p. 73.

53 There are no definitive national figures available, and
    residency varies by institution and time, so a precise
    count is difficult. A large metropolitan institution such
    as the University of Sydney currently houses 5 per cent of
    students on campus, and the University of Melbourne hosts
    5.7 per cent of students in colleges.

54 In a personal communication, in 2017, Simon Marginson
    observes that the 'always present' comprehensive nature
    of Australian universities 'coincides with the main line
    of international development, in the direction of the
    comprehensive multi-disciplinary multi-purpose university.
    This has been a significant factor in the high global
    performance—on a modest public financing base—of
    Australian universities'.

55 Turney, Bygott and Chippendale, *Australia's First*, p. 123.

56 In ibid., p. 116. Italics in original.

57 Newman, *The Idea of a University*, Preface, p. 3. Reading
    The Idea is a very big commitment. As Dr Johnson said of
    Paradise Lost, this is 'one of the books which the reader
    admires and lays down, and forgets to take up again. None
    ever wished it longer than it is'.

58 In Anderson, *European Universities from the
    Enlightenment to 1914*, 2004, p. 55.

59 Connell et al., *Australia's First: A History of the University
    of Sydney, Vol. 2: 1940–1990*, 1995, quoted by Forsyth,
    'Disinterested Scholars or Interested Parties? The Public's
    Investment in Self-interested Universities', in Thornton
    (ed.), *Through a Glass Darkly: The Social Sciences Look at
    the Neoliberal University*, p. 28.

60 Blainey, *A Centenary History of the University of
    Melbourne*, 1957, p. 196.

61 Alas, needless to say, this excluded all those without
    access to reasonable secondary education, such as most
    Indigenous people. See Horne and Sherington, *Sydney: The
    Making of a Public University*, pp. 53–7.

62 Horne and Sherington, *Sydney: The Making of a Public
    University*, and in personal communication, 2017. See
    also Horne and Sherington, 'Extending the Educational
    Franchise', p. 209, and Horne, Campbell and Sherington,
    'The Idea of the University in the British Colonies', 2007.

63 'Though the constellation is changed, the disposition is the
    same.' Clive James renders the motto as: 'Sydney University
    is really Oxford or Cambridge laterally displaced
    approximately 12,000 miles'. James, *Unreliable Memoirs*,
    1980, p. 125.

64 Cable, 'Woolley, John (1816–1866)'.

65 Selleck, *The Shop*, pp. 14–15.
66 Ibid., p. 20.
67 Ibid., pp. 52, 55.
68 Personal communication, 2017, from university historian Carolyn Rasmussen.
69 Horne and Sherington, 'Extending the Educational Franchise', pp. 209–210.
70 Selleck, *The Shop*, p. 147; Blainey, *A Centenary History of the University of Melbourne*, p. 48.
71 Selleck, *The Shop*, p. 111.
72 Pietsch, *Empire of Scholars*, p. 79.
73 See Henningham, 'Weir, Margaret Williams', *Encyclopedia of Women & Leadership in Twentieth-Century Australia*, 2014.
74 Pietsch, *Empire of Scholars*, p. 79.
75 Davis, *Open to Talent: The Centenary History of the University of Tasmania 1890–1990*, 1990, pp. 17–18.
76 Thomis, *A Place of Light & Learning: The University of Queensland's First Seventy-five Years*, 1985, p. 21.
77 Byers and Thackrah, 'Constructing the Student Experience', in Gregory with Chetkovich (eds), *Seeking Wisdom: A Centenary History of the University of Western Australia*, 2013, p. 184.
78 Linn, *The Spirit of Knowledge*, pp. 14–15.
79 Turney, Bygott and Chippendale, *Australia's First*, p. 134.
80 Selleck, *The Shop*, p. 27.
81 Thrift says that 'universities, like most institutions, have accreted new values (and thrown others aside) as they have acquired new strands of activity'. 'The University of Life', p. 400.
82 In Collini, *What Are Universities for?*, p. 21.

3   Attempts to leave the path

1   Jordan, *A Spirit of True Learning: The Jubilee History of the University of New England*, 2004, pp. 15, 78, 98.
2   Castle, *University of Wollongong: An Illustrated History 1951–1991*, 1991, pp. 3, 11.
3   University of New South Wales—University Archives, *Broken Hill Division of the University of New South Wales*, 2014.

4   Queensland, Legislative Assembly, *Parliamentary Debates*,
    3 November 1959, pp. 1088–9.
5   Foster and Varghese, *The Making of the Australian
    National University, 1946–1996*, 1996, pp. 4–5.
6   Ibid., pp. 13, 21, 38.
7   *The Australian National University Act 1946*, S6 (a).
8   Foster and Varghese, *The Making of the Australian
    National University*, p. 3.
9   Ibid., p. 180.
10 *Technical Education and New South Wales University of
    Technology Act 1949*, S18.
11 O'Farrell, *UNSW, a Portrait: The University of New South
    Wales 1949–1999*, 1999, p. 75.
12 *Report of the Committee on Australian Universities* (The
    Murray Report), 1957, p. 88.
13 University of New South Wales, *History*, 2017.
14 Davison and Murphy, *University Unlimited: The Monash
    Story*, 2012, p. 5.
15 Mr Sutton spoke in a debate on the Monash University
    Bill, see Victoria, Legislative Assembly, *Parliamentary
    Debates*, 1 April 1958, p. 3935.
16 *Report of the Committee on Australian Universities*
    (The Murray Report), p. 87.
17 In Davison and Murphy, *University Unlimited*, p. 55.
18 Foster and Varghese, *The Making of the Australian
    National University*, p. 201.
19 Davison and Murphy, *University Unlimited*, p. 137.
20 Perry, *The Rise and Fall of Practically Everybody: An
    Account of Student Political Activity at Monash University,
    1965–1972*, 1973, p. 4, in Davison and Murphy,
    University Unlimited, p. 118.
21 James, *Unreliable Memoirs*, p. 127.
22 Personal communication from Howard Whitton in 2017,
    who attended the 1974 seminar as a ministerial liaison
    officer for then Education Minister Kim E Beazley. This
    was not a phenomenon unique to the 1960s. Two decades
    earlier, reports Donald Horne, 'I had been moved by
    McAuley's prose piece in *Hermes* about how he went
    home, but could not talk to his parents, and went away
    again', *The Education of Young Donald*, 1967, p. 238.

23 Personal communication from Ian Marshman, 2017.

24 Mansfield and Hutchinson, *Liberality of Opportunity: A History of Macquarie University 1964–1989*, 1992, p. 30.

25 In ibid., pp. 31, 51.

26 In ibid., p. 55.

27 A quote from a letter by Robert Springborg to Vice-Chancellor Di Yerbury in November 1989, in ibid., p. 289.

28 I here draw on Davis, 'Making the World Safe for Diversity: Forty Years of Higher Education', *Australian Book Review*, March 2007, which is an expanded version of the inaugural ABR/Flinders University Annual Lecture, delivered in 2006.

29 Flinders University, *Peter Karmel Memorial Booklet*, 2009.

30 Hilliard, *Flinders University: The First 25 Years, 1966–1991*, 1991, p. 29.

31 Ibid., pp. 110–11.

32 Manne, 'An Academic's Dozen', in La Trobe University (ed.), *From the Paddock to the Agora: Fifty Years of La Trobe University*, 2017, p. 54.

33 Watson, 'Goodness and Wisdom in Bundoora', in La Trobe University (ed.), *From the Paddock to the Agora*, p. 29.

34 Miller, 'Murdoch's Trajectory: From Periphery to Core; From Core to Periphery?', in Murdoch University (ed.), *Murdoch Voices: The First 40 Years at Murdoch University*, 2015.

35 Geoffrey Bolton reports that when Murdoch (at this point frail, ill and in his nineties) was asked by the state government about their intention to name a second university in WA after him, Murdoch 'was moved: what a marvellous tribute, he murmured, yes of course he was agreeable. Then a pause, and a glint of the essential Walter Murdoch: "But it had better be a good one."' Bolton, *It Had Better Be a Good One: The First Ten Years of Murdoch University*, 1985, p. 7.

36 Ibid., p. 30.

37 Ibid., pp. 53–4.

38 Byers and Thackrah, 'Constructing the Student Experience', in Gregory with Chetkovich (eds), *Seeking Wisdom: A Centenary History of the University of Western Australia*, 2013, pp. 161–2.

39 University of Western Australia, 'How Many Students Does It Take to Dig a Hole?', *Stories from the Archives*, 2015.

40 Bolton, *It Had Better Be a Good One*, p. 56. See also Wackett, 'Theme and Variations—Music at Murdoch', in Murdoch University (ed.), *Murdoch Voices*, p. 122.

41 Macmillan, *Australian Universities: A Descriptive Sketch*, 1968, p. 85; DEETYA, *Selected Higher Education Staff Statistics, 1997*, 1997. Of course, there are many myths about who worked at universities. A character in Laurie Clancy's *The Wildlife Reserve* reminisces about the 1960s, a time when a job at a university was said to be easy: 'Anybody could get a job in a university then. We had one chap come out to wash the windows of the Arts building. He stayed on to become the first Professor of Sociology. Many was the story of a young man's meteoric rise to mediocrity'. 1994, p. 62.

42 Quirke, *Preparing for the Future: A History of Griffith University 1971–1996*, 1996. p. 11.

43 Fitzgerald, *Pushed From the Wings: An Entertainment*, 1986.

4   A unified national system

1   Rayson, *Life after George*, 2000. The description of the play is drawn from the introduction by Peter Craven, and this dialogue from pp. 58–9.

2   Macintyre, *Australia's Boldest Experiment: War and Reconstruction in the 1940s*, 2015, pp. 214–15, 459.

3   Australia, House of Representatives, *Parliamentary Debates*, 23 November 1960, p. 3.

4   Macintyre, with Croucher, Davis and Marginson, 'Making the Unified National System', in Croucher et al. (eds), *The Dawkins Revolution: 25 Years On*, 2013, p. 21. Stuart quotes Dawkins, *The Challenge for Higher Education in Australia*, 1987, p. 2.

5   The material that follows is informed closely by *No End of a Lesson*, a study of the Dawkins reforms by Macintyre, Brett and Croucher (2017), and the earlier volume *The Dawkins Revolution*, edited by Croucher et al. *No End of a Lesson* is one of the outcomes of an ARC Discovery

project on the history of the Unified National System,
DP140102874.

6   Personal communication from Simon Marginson, 2017.

7   Macintyre, 'Making the Unified National System', p.17.

8   'The number of institutions providing higher education
    dropped from 73 in 1987 (not counting TAFEs) with an
    average size of 5,300 students, to 38 in 1991 with an
    average of 14,000 students.' DET, *Higher Education in
    Australia: A Review of Reviews from Dawkins to Today*,
    2015, p. 12.

9   A process described with clarity and humour in Alison
    Mackinnon's *A New Kid on the Block: The University of
    South Australia in the Unified National System*, 2016.

10 The comma after Technology was dropped by UTS in
    2015. See Loussikian, 'UTS Banishes Comma that Made It
    an "Orphan"', *The Australian*, 8 July 2015.

11 Vin Massaro was Director of Administration and Registrar
    at Flinders University. See his address to the AITEA (SA)
    Branch, 'Mergers—the Government's Intentions and Likely
    Outcomes', 1989.

12 Brett, Croucher and Macintyre, *Life after Dawkins: The
    University of Melbourne in the Unified National System of
    Higher Education*, 2016, pp. 44–5.

13 Horne and Garton, *Preserving the Past: The University
    of Sydney and the Unified National System of Higher
    Education 1987–96*, 2017, p. 140.

14 Ibid., pp. 140–3. In *Liberal Education and Useful
    Knowledge: A Brief History of the University of Sydney
    1850–2000*, 2002, p. 43, Williams concurs: 'It was a
    "brave" decision and one that created problems that were
    much greater than those arising from the amalgamations
    agreed to by the universities of Melbourne, Adelaide,
    Western Australia, Queensland and New South Wales.
    As judged by the indicators widely used, the University of
    Sydney fell in rank'.

15 Page, 'Path Dependence', *Quarterly Journal of Political
    Science*, 2006, p. 88.

16 Massaro, 'Mergers—the Government's Intentions and
    Likely Outcomes'.

17 Foster and Varghese, *The Making of the Australian National University, 1946–1996*, 1996, p. 342.
18 Massaro, *Developing Diversity*, 1995, pp. 5–6.
19 For example Meyers, *Australian Universities: A Portrait of Decline*, 2012.
20 Horne, *Into the Open: Memoirs 1958–1999*, 2000, p. 226.
21 In Epstein, 'Lower Education: Sex Toys and Academic Freedom at Northwestern', *Weekly Standard*, 21 March 2011.
22 Universities Australia, *Higher Education and Research Facts and Figures: November 2015*, 2015.
23 A case argued eloquently by Ben Etherington in 'This Little University Went to Market', *Sydney Review of Books*, 21 June 2016.
24 'ABC Fact Check calculated there were 13 students for every teacher in 1990. The number rose to 19 in 2000 and 24 in 2012.' ABC Fact Check, 'National Tertiary Education Union Correct on University Class Sizes', *ABC News*, 30 August 2013.
25 Specifically, this was 56 per cent, according to Andrews et al., *Contingent Academic Employment in Australian Universities*, 2016, p. 1.
26 Collini, 'Sold Out', *London Review of Books*, 5 December 2013.
27 Jayasuriya, 'Transforming the Public University: Market Citizenship and Higher Education Regulatory Projects', in Thornton (ed.), *Through a Glass Darkly: The Social Sciences Look at the Neoliberal University*, 2014, p. 99.
28 Marginson and Considine, *The Enterprise University: Power, Governance and Reinvention in Australia*, 2000, p. 175.
29 Ibid., pp. 188–90.
30 Ibid., p. 185. In a personal communication in 2017, Sharon Bell notes that institutional differences can be deeply local, citing a study of the Physics Department at UNSW. This suggested that the lived experience of women in Physics in one place was different from that of their male counterparts, and from women elsewhere in the same institution.

31 van Vught, 'Mission Diversity and Reputation in Higher
     Education', *Higher Education Policy*, 2008.
32 DiMaggio and Powell, 'The Iron Cage Revisited:
     Institutional Isomorphism and Collective Rationality in
     Organizational Fields', *American Sociological Review*,
     1983, p. 147.
33 Rosen, *Change.edu: Rebooting for the New Talent
     Economy*, 2011, p. xvii.
34 Marginson and Considine, *The Enterprise University*,
     p. 184.
35 A process described in Massaro, 'New Quality Assurance
     Frameworks for Higher Education: Quality Assurance in
     Transnational Education', 1999, pp. 6–7.
36 Norton and Cakitaki, *Mapping Australian Higher
     Education 2016*, 2016, p. 15.
37 In Dodd, 'John Dawkins Throws Down the Challenge to
     Labor on University reform', *Australian Financial Review*,
     26 September 2016.

5 What next?

1   Coates et al., *Profiling Diversity of Australian Universities*,
     June 2013.
2   In 'Political Ideology in Australia: The Distinctiveness
     of a Benthamite Society', *Daedalus*, 1985, Hugh Collins
     calls this a 'Benthamite' view of the world. Following the
     philosophy of Jeremy Bentham, Collins argues, Australian
     political settlements tend to be utilitarian because
     concerned to maximise outcomes for most citizens, legalist
     because purpose and organisational form are defined by
     legislation rather than trusted to custom, and positivist
     because Australia's public institutions express a practical
     ambition, focused on outcomes rather than speculation
     about principle.
3   Noonan, 'Australian HE Reforms Need Further Vetting',
     Times Higher Education, 22 June 2017; Noonan, 'The
     Current and Future Landscape for Tertiary Education
     Funding', *The Mandarin*, 26 July 2017.
4   Emison, *Degrees for a New Generation*, 2013.
5   Whitehead, *Science and the Modern World*, 1938
     (f.p. 1926), p. 240.

6   van Vught, 'Mission Diversity and Reputation in Higher
      Education', *Higher Education Policy*, 2008, p. 151, abstract.
7   In Pelikan, *The Idea of the University—A Re-examination*,
      1992, p. 13.
8   To date, relatively few Australian students study for
      degrees offshore, though study abroad for a semester or a
      year is popular. A 2017 report noted that in 2014 '11,447
      Australian students enrolled in tertiary courses in other
      countries'. While significant and growing, at this stage
      the number of Australians choosing universities outside
      the nation is about 0.01 per cent of the local education
      load. DET, *International Mobility of Australian University
      Students*, January 2017.
9   DET, 'Chinese Universities Establishing Programs and
      Campuses in Foreign Countries', undated.
10   Wildavsky, *The Great Brain Race: How Global
      Universities Are Reshaping the World*, 2010.
11   Howarth, 'The Business of Higher Education', *Australia
      Unlimited*, 13 August 2015; Norton, Sonnemann and
      McGannon, *The Online Evolution: When Technology
      Meets Tradition in Higher Education*, 2013, pp. 7, 9
      and 16.
12   Norton and Cakitaki, *Mapping Australian Higher
      Education 2016*, 2016, p. 10. Forty-three of the 170 are
      universities.
13   Marginson, 'The Impossibility of Capitalist Markets in
      Higher Education', *Journal of Education Policy*, 2013,
      p. 353, abstract.
14   In Macintyre, Brett and Croucher, *No End of a Lesson:
      Australia's Unified National System of Higher Education*,
      2017, p. 154.
15   Marginson, 'Dynamics of National and Global
      Competition in Higher Education', *Higher Education*,
      2006.
16   Universities Australia, *Offshore Programs of Australian
      Universities*, April 2014.
17   O'Keefe, 'UNSW Singapore Campus Doomed to Fail', *The
      Australian*, 27 June 2007.
18   Marginson, *The Dream Is Over: The Crisis of Clark Kerr's
      California Idea of Higher Education*, 2016, p. 78.

19 Lacy et al., *Australian Universities at a Crossroads: Insights from Their Leaders and Implications for the Future*, 2017, p. 47.

20 Trow, 'Elite and Mass Higher Education: American Models and European Realities', in Swedish National Board of Universities and Colleges (ed.), *Research into Higher Education: Processes and Structures. Information on Higher Education in Sweden*, 1979. See also van Vught, 'Mission Diversity and Reputation in Higher Education', p. 21.

21 Noonan, 'The Current and Future Landscape for Tertiary Education Funding'.

22 Lacy et al., *Australian Universities at a Crossroads*, p. 49.

23 Wolf, 'Degrees of Failure: Why It's Time to Reconsider How We Run Our Universities', Prospect, 14 July 2017.

24 This account is drawn from my experience as an international member of the UGC 2008–2011.

25 Coaldrake and Stedman, *Raising the Stakes: Gambling with the Future of Universities*, 2016, p. 273.

26 Anderson, 'The "Idea of a University" Today', *History and Policy*, 1 March 2010.

27 DEETYA, *Learning for Life: Review of Higher Education Financing and Policy: Final Report*, 1998, p. 88.

28 Bebbington, 'Is the Traditional Research University Doomed to Extinction in a Digital Age?', *Times Higher Education*, 20 April 2017.

29 Garner, *The Student Chronicles*, 2006, p. 152.

30 Massaro, 'Diversity Must Be Rewarded', *The Australian*, 16 July 2003.

BIBLIOGRAPHY

ABC Fact Check, 'National Tertiary Education Union Correct on University Class Sizes', *ABC News*, 30 August 2013. http://www.abc.net.au/news/factcheck/2013-08-30/ nteu-correct-on-university-class-sizes/4917678 (viewed June 2017).

Anderson, Hephzibah, 'Why Is QWERTY on Our Keyboards?', *BBC Culture*, 13 December 2016. http://www.bbc.com/ culture/story/20161212-why-is-qwerty-on-our-keyboards (viewed May 2017).

Anderson, Robert D, *European Universities from the Enlightenment to 1914*, Oxford University Press, Oxford, 2004.

—— 'The "Idea of a University" Today', *History and Policy*, 1 March 2010. http://www.historyandpolicy.org/policy-papers/papers/the-idea-of-a-university-today (viewed May 2017).

Andrews, Stuart, Liz Bare, Peter Bentley, Leo Goedegebuure, Catherine Pugsley and Bianca Rance, *Contingent Academic Employment in Australian Universities*, LH Martin Institute and the Australian Higher Education Industrial Association, 2016. http://www.lhmartininstitute.edu. au/documents/publications/2016-contingent-academic-employment-in-australian-universities-updatedapr16.pdf (viewed May 2017).

Atkinson, Alan, '"Do Unto Others": Australia and the Anglican Conscience, 1840–56 and Afterwards', in S Macintyre, L Layman and J Gregory (eds), *A Historian for All Seasons: Essays for Geoffrey Bolton*, Monash University Publishing, Clayton, 2017, pp. 113–40.

Australia, House of Representatives, *Parliamentary Debates*, 23 November 1960, p. 3.

Backus, John, 'Commentary: Creative Destruction Meets Higher Education', *The Washington Post*, 19 May 2013. https://www.washingtonpost.com/business/capitalbusiness/commentary-creative-destruction-meets-higher-education/2013/05/17/f8b3bcd6-bbe3-11e2-97d4-a479289a31f9_story.html (viewed May 2017).

Bebbington, Warren, 'Is the Traditional Research University Doomed to Extinction in a Digital Age?', *Times Higher Education*, 20 April 2017. https://www.timeshighereducation.com/features/traditional-research-university-doomed-extinction-digital-age (viewed June 2017).

Blainey, Geoffrey, *A Centenary History of the University of Melbourne*, Melbourne University Press, Carlton, 1957.

Bolton, Geoffrey, *It Had Better Be a Good One: The First Ten Years of Murdoch University*, Murdoch University, Perth, 1985.

Brett, André, Gwilym Croucher and Stuart Macintyre, *Life after Dawkins: The University of Melbourne in the Unified National System of Higher Education*, Melbourne University Publishing, Carlton, 2016.

Byers, Susie and Andrew Thackrah, 'Constructing the Student Experience', in J Gregory with J Chetkovich (eds), *Seeking Wisdom: A Centenary History of the University of Western Australia*, UWA Publishing, Crawley, 2013, pp. 159–96.

Cable, Kenneth J, 'Woolley, John (1816–1866)', *Australian Dictionary of Biography*, vol. 6, Melbourne University Publishing, Carlton, 1976. http://adb.anu.edu.au/biography/woolley-john-4885 (viewed July 2017).

Cable, Kenneth, Clifford Turney and Ursula Bygott, *Australia's First: A Pictorial History of the University of Sydney 1850–1990*, University of Sydney, Sydney, 1994.

Carnegie Classification of Institutions of Higher Education, 'Basic Classification Description', 2017. http://carnegieclassifications.iu.edu/classification_descriptions/basic.php (viewed May 2017).

Castle, Josie, *University of Wollongong: An illustrated History 1951–1991*, University of Wollongong, Wollongong, 1991.

Clancy, Laurie, *The Wildlife Reserve*, Angus & Robertson, Sydney, 1994.

Coaldrake, Peter and Lawrence Stedman, *Raising the Stakes: Gambling with the Future of Universities*, University of Queensland Press, Brisbane, 2016.

Coates, Hamish, Daniel Edwards, Leo Goedegebuure, Marian Thakur, Eva van der Brugge and Frans van Vught, *Profiling Diversity of Australian Universities*, Research Briefing, LH Martin Institute and ACER, June 2013.

Cohan, Peter, 'Why Peter Thiel Is Wrong to Pay Students to Drop Out', *Forbes*, 15 June 2011. https://www.forbes.com/sites/petercohan/2011/06/15/why-peter-thiel-is-wrong-to-pay-students-to-drop-out/#5342e3534ac3 (viewed May 2017).

Collini, Stefan, 'From Robbins to McKinsey', *London Review of Books*, vol. 33, no. 16, 25 August 2011, pp. 9–14. https://www.lrb.co.uk/v33/n16/stefan-collini/from-robbins-to-mckinsey (viewed May 2017).

—— *What Are Universities for?*, Penguin UK, London, 2012.

—— 'Sold Out', *London Review of Books*, vol. 35, no. 20, 5 December 2013, pp. 3–12. https://www.lrb.co.uk/v35/n20/stefan-collini/sold-out (viewed July 2017).

Collins, Hugh, 'Political Ideology in Australia: The Distinctiveness of a Benthamite Society', *Daedalus*, vol. 114, no. 1, Australia: Terra Incognita?, Winter, 1985, pp. 147–69.

Colony of New South Wales Legislative Council, *Votes and Proceedings*, Friday 28 June 1850, p. 44.

—— *An Act to Incorporate and Endow the University of Sydney*, 1 October 1850. http://www.legislation.nsw.gov.au/acts/1850-31a.pdf (viewed May 2017).

Connell, William F, Geoffrey Sherington, Brian H Fletcher, Clifford Turney and Ursula Bygott, *Australia's First: A History of the University of Sydney, Vol. 2: 1940–1990*, Hale & Iremonger, Sydney, 1995.

Croucher, Gwilym, Simon Marginson, Andrew Norton and Julie Wells (eds), *The Dawkins Revolution: 25 Years on*, Melbourne University Publishing, Carlton, 2013.

David, Paul A, 'Clio and the Economics of QWERTY', *The American Economic Review*, vol. 75, no. 2, 1985, pp. 332–7.

Davis, Glyn, 'The Rising Phoenix of Competition: What Future for Australia's Public Universities?', *Griffith Review*, Autumn, 2006, pp. 15–31.

—— 'Making the World Safe for Diversity: Forty Years of Higher Education', *Australian Book Review*, March 2007, pp. 28–34 (expanded version of the inaugural *ABR/* Flinders University Annual Lecture, 2006).

—— *The Republic of Learning: Higher Education Transforms Australia*, The Boyer Lecture Series 2010, Harper Collins Publishers, Sydney, 2010.

—— 'The Australian Idea of a University', *Meanjin*, vol. 72, no. 3, 2013, pp. 32–48.

Davis, Richard, *Open to Talent: The Centenary History of the University of Tasmania 1890–1990*, University of Tasmania, Hobart, 1990.

Davison, Graeme and Kate Murphy, *University Unlimited: The Monash Story*, Allen & Unwin, Sydney, 2012.

Dawkins, John S, *The Challenge for Higher Education in Australia*, AGPS, Canberra, September 1987.

Department of Education and Training (DET), *Higher Education in Australia: A Review of Reviews from Dawkins to Today*, Department of Education and Training, Canberra, 2015.

—— *International Mobility of Australian University Students*, Research Snapshot, January 2017. https:// internationaleducation.gov.au/research/Research-Snapshots/Documents/Outgoing%20international%20 mobility_HE_2015.pdf (viewed May 2017).

—— 'Chinese Universities Establishing Programs and Campuses in Foreign Countries', Canberra, undated. https:// internationaleducation.gov.au/News/Latest-News/Pages/ Chinese-universities-establishing.aspx (viewed May 2017).

Department of Employment, Education, Training and Youth Affairs (DEETYA), *Selected Higher Education Staff Statistics, 1997*, Commonwealth of Australia, Canberra, 1997.

—— *Learning for Life: Review of Higher Education Financing and Policy: Final Report*, Commonwealth of Australia, Canberra, 1998.

DiMaggio, Paul J and Walter W Powell, 'The Iron Cage Revisited: Institutional Isomorphism and Collective

Rationality in Organizational Fields', *American
Sociological Review*, vol. 48, April 1983, pp. 147–60.

Dodd, Tim, 'John Dawkins Throws Down the Challenge to
Labor on University Reform', *Australian Financial Review*,
26 September 2016. http://www.afr.com/news/politics/
national/john-dawkins-throws-down-the-challenge-to-labor-
on-university-reform-20160922-grmii0 (viewed July 2017).

—— 'New Study Reveals $40 Billion Is Invested in Education
Technology', *Australian Financial Review*, 8 May 2017,
p. 12.

The Economist, 'Higher Education: Creative Destruction',
28 June 2014. http://www.economist.com/news/
leaders/21605906-cost-crisis-changing-labour-markets-and-
new-technology-will-turn-old-institution-its (viewed May
2017).

—— 'Established Education Providers v New Contenders:
Alternative Providers of Education Must Solve the
Problems of Cost and Credentials', Special report,
12 January 2017. https://www.economist.com/news/
special-report/21714173-alternative-providers-education-
must-solve-problems-cost-and (viewed August 2017).

Eldredge, Niles and Stephen J Gould, 'Punctuated Equilibria:
An Alternative to Phyletic Gradualism', in TJM Schopf
(ed.), *Models in Paleobiology*, Freeman Cooper, San
Francisco, 1972, pp. 82–115.

Emison, Mary, *Degrees for a New Generation*, Melbourne
University Press, Carlton, 2013.

Epstein, Joseph, 'Lower Education: Sex Toys and Academic
Freedom at Northwestern', *Weekly Standard*, vol. 16,
no. 26, 21 March 2011. http://www.weeklystandard.com/
lower-education/article/554092 (viewed July 2017).

Etherington, Ben, 'This Little University Went to Market',
Sydney Review of Books, 21 June 2016. http://
sydneyreviewofbooks.com/little-university-went-market/
(viewed May 2017).

Fain, Paul, 'Fine Print and Tough Questions for the Purdue–
Kaplan Deal', *Inside Higher Ed*, 30 May 2017. https://
www.insidehighered.com/news/2017/05/30/regulators-and-
accreditor-begin-review-purdues-boundary-testing-deal-
kaplan?mc_cid=f8d01f6238&mc_eid=55d45fedc2 (viewed
June 2017).

Fitzgerald, Ross, *Pushed from the Wings: An Entertainment*, Hale & Iremonger, Sydney, 1986.

Flinders University, *Peter Karmel Memorial Booklet*, 2009. http://issuu.com/flindersuniversity/docs/karmel_memorial_ booklet (viewed May 2017).

Forsyth, Hannah, 'Disinterested Scholars or Interested Parties? The Public's Investment in Self-interested Universities', in M Thornton (ed.), *Through a Glass Darkly: The Social Sciences Look at the Neoliberal University*, ANU Press, Canberra, 2014, pp. 19–36.

Foster, Stephen G and Margaret M Varghese, *The Making of the Australian National University, 1946–1996*, Allen & Unwin, Sydney, 1996.

Garner, Alice, *The Student Chronicles*, The Miegunyah Press, Carlton, 2006.

Henningham, Nikki, 'Weir, Margaret Williams', *Encyclopedia of Women & Leadership in Twentieth-Century Australia*, 2014. http://www.womenaustralia.info/leaders/biogs/ WLE0768b.htm (viewed May 2017).

Hilliard, David, *Flinders University: The First 25 Years, 1966–1991*, The Flinders University of South Australia, Adelaide, 1991.

Hinrichs, Peter L, *Trends in Employment at US Colleges and Universities, 1987–2013*, Federal Reserve Bank of Cleveland, 2016. https://clevelandfed. org/newsroom-and-events/publications/economic- commentary/2016-economic-commentaries/ec-201605- trends-in-employment-at-us-colleges-and-universities.aspx (viewed June 2017).

Hirst, John, *Freedom on the Fatal Shore: Australia's First Colony*, Black Inc., Carlton, 2008.

Horne, Donald, *The Education of Young Donald*, Angus & Robertson, Sydney, 1967.

—— *Into the Open: Memoirs 1958–1999*, Harper Collins, Sydney, 2000.

Horne, Julia, 'Political Machinations and Sectarian Intrigue in the Making of Sydney University', *Journal of the Australian Catholic Historical Society*, vol. 36, 2015, pp. 4–15.

Horne, Julia, Roderic Campbell and Geoffrey Sherington, 'The Idea of the University in the British Colonies', paper presented at the International Conference on the Quest for

Excellence: Great Universities and their Cities, Mumbai,
     Kolkata and Chennai, Mumbai, 17–19 January 2007.
Horne, Julia and Stephen Garton, *Preserving the Past: The
     University of Sydney and the Unified National System
     of Higher Education 1987–96*, Melbourne University
     Publishing, Carlton, 2017.
Horne, Julia and Geoffrey Sherington, 'Extending the
     Educational Franchise: The Social Contract of Australia's
     Public Universities, 1850–1890', *Paedagogica Historica*,
     vol. 46, no. 1, 2010, pp. 207–27.
—— *Sydney: The Making of a Public University*, The
     Miegunyah Press, Carlton, 2012.
—— '"Dominion Legacies": The Case of Australia', in D
     Schreuder (ed.), *Universities for a New World: Making
     an International Network in Global Higher Education,
     1913–2013*, Sage, India, 2013, pp. 284–307.
Howarth, Brad, 'The Business of Higher Education', *Australia
     Unlimited*, Austrade, 13 August 2015. https://www.
     australiaunlimited.com/technology/the-business-of-
     distance-education (viewed May 2017).
Ignatieff, Michael, *Isaiah Berlin: A Life*, Vintage, London, 1998.
James, Clive, *Unreliable Memoirs*, Jonathan Cape, London,
     1980.
Jayasuriya, Kanishka, 'Transforming the Public University:
     Market Citizenship and Higher Education Regulatory
     Projects', in M Thornton (ed.), *Through a Glass Darkly:
     The Social Sciences Look at the Neoliberal University*,
     ANU Press, Canberra, 2014, pp. 89–102.
Jordan, Matthew, *A Spirit of True Learning: The Jubilee
     History of the University of New England*, UNSW Press,
     Sydney, 2004.
Kao, John, *Innovation Nation*, Free Press, New York, 2007.
Kerr, Clark, *The Uses of the University*, 5th edn, Harvard
     University Press, Cambridge, MA, 2001.
Lacy, William B, Gwilym Croucher, André Brett and Romina
     Mueller, *Australian Universities at a Crossroads: Insights
     from Their Leaders and Implications for the Future*,
     University of Melbourne Centre of Higher Education and
     Berkeley Centre for Studies in Higher Education, 2017.
Lange, Julian, Edward Marram and William Bygrave, 'Human
     Assets and Entrepreneurial Performance: A Study of

Companies Started by Business School Graduates', *Journal of Business and Entrepreneurship*, vol. 24, no. 1, 2012, pp. 1–24.

Leckart, S, 'The Stanford Education Experiment Could Change Higher Learning Forever', *Wired*, 20 March 2012. https://www.wired.com/2012/03/ff_aiclass/ (viewed May 2017).

Liebowitz, Stan J and Stephen E Margolis, 'The Fable of the Keys', in D Spulber (ed.), *Famous Fables of Economics*, Blackwell Publishers, Malden, MA, 2002, originally in *Journal of Law and Economics*, vol. 30, no. 1, April 1990, pp. 1–26.

Linn, Rob, *The Spirit of Knowledge: A Social History of the University of Adelaide North Terrace Campus*, Barr Smith Press, Adelaide, 2011.

Longo, Donato, 'History Honours, 1901–2010', in W Prest (ed.), *Pasts Present: History at Australia's Third University*, Wakefield Press, Adelaide, 2014, pp. 116–29.

Loussikian, Kylar, 'UTS Banishes Comma that Made It an "Orphan"', *The Australian*, 8 July 2015. http://www.theaustralian.com.au/higher-education/uts-banishes-comma-that-made-it-an-orphan/news-story/a55db6ea0f2573081fc01b218b3f08c6 (viewed June 2017).

McCord, Norman and Bill Purdue, *British History 1815–1914*, Oxford University Press, Oxford, 2007.

Macintyre, Stuart, *Australia's Boldest Experiment: War and Reconstruction in the 1940s*, NewSouth, Sydney, 2015.

Macintyre, Stuart, André Brett and Gwilym Croucher, *No End of a Lesson: Australia's Unified National System of Higher Education*, Melbourne University Publishing, Carlton, 2017.

Macintyre, Stuart, with Gwilym Croucher, Glyn Davis and Simon Marginson, 'Making the Unified National System', in G Croucher, S Marginson, A Norton and J Wells (eds), *The Dawkins Revolution: 25 Years On*, Melbourne University Publishing, Carlton, 2013, pp. 9–55.

Mackinnon, Alison, *A New Kid on the Block: The University of South Australia in the Unified National System*, Melbourne University Publishing, Carlton, 2016.

Macmillan, David, *Australian Universities: A Descriptive Sketch*, Sydney University Press for Australian Vice-Chancellors' Committee, Sydney, 1968.

Manne, Robert, 'An Academic's Dozen', in La Trobe University
    (ed.), *From the Paddock to the Agora: Fifty Years of La
    Trobe University*, La Trobe University in conjunction with
    Black Inc., Carlton, 2017, pp. 37–55.
Mansfield, Bruce and Mark Hutchinson, *Liberality of
    Opportunity: A History of Macquarie University 1964–
    1989*, Macquarie University in association with Hale &
    Iremonger, Sydney, 1992.
Marginson, Simon, 'Dynamics of National and Global
    Competition in Higher Education', *Higher Education*, vol.
    52, no. 1, 2006, pp. 1–39.
—— 'The Impossibility of Capitalist Markets in Higher
    Education', *Journal of Education Policy*, vol. 28, no. 3,
    2013, pp. 353–70.
—— *The Dream Is Over: The Crisis of Clark Kerr's California
    Idea of Higher Education*, University of California Press,
    Oakland, CA, 2016.
Marginson, Simon and Mark Considine, *The Enterprise
    University: Power, Governance and Reinvention in
    Australia*, Cambridge University Press, Melbourne, 2000.
Massaro, Vin, 'Mergers—the Government's Intentions and
    Likely Outcomes', Address to the AITEA (SA) Branch,
    16 August 1989.
—— *Developing Diversity*, Organisation for Economic
    Co-operation and Development, Programme on
    Institutional Management in Higher Education,
    Institutional Responses to Quality Assessment Seminar,
    Paris, 4–6 December 1995.
—— 'New Quality Assurance Frameworks for Higher
    Education: Quality Assurance in Transnational Education',
    Address to the Tertiary Education Managers Annual
    Conference, Wellington, 26–29 September 1999.
—— 'Diversity Must Be Rewarded', *The Australian*, 16 July
    2003.
Matchett, Stephen, 'Uni Lobby Laments: We're Being Punished
    for Peak Performance', *Campus Morning Mail*, 4 May
    2017. http://campusmorningmail.com.au/uni-lobby-
    laments-were-being-punished-for-peak-performance/
    (viewed May 2017).
Meyers, Donald, *Australian Universities: A Portrait of Decline*,
    AUPOD, Brisbane, 2012.

Mill, John Stuart, 'Inaugural Address to the University of St
    Andrews', 1867, in JM Robson (ed.), *The Collected Works
    of John Stuart Mill, Vol. XXI—Essays on Equality, Law,
    and Education*, University of Toronto Press, Toronto,
    1984.

Miller, Toby, 'Murdoch's Trajectory: From Periphery to
    Core; From Core to Periphery?', in Murdoch University
    (ed.), *Murdoch Voices: The First 40 Years at Murdoch
    University*, Murdoch University, Perth, 2015, pp. 88–93.

Murdoch University (ed.), *Murdoch Voices: The First 40 Years
    at Murdoch University*, Murdoch University, Perth, 2015.

Newman, John H, *The Idea of a University Defined and
    Illustrated: In Nine Discourses Delivered to the Catholics
    of Dublin*, Yale University Press, New Haven, 1996 (f.p.
    1852).

—— *Historical Sketches*, vol. 3, Longmans, Green, and Co.,
    London, 1889.

Noonan, Peter, 'Australian HE Reforms Need Further Vetting',
    Times Higher Education, 22 June 2017. https://www.
    timeshighereducation.com/opinion/australian-he-reforms-
    need-further-vetting (viewed July 2017).

—— 'The Current and Future Landscape for Tertiary Education
    Funding', *The Mandarin*, 26 July 2017. http://www.
    themandarin.com.au/81818-the-current-and-future-
    landscape-for-tertiary-education-funding/ (viewed
    July 2017).

Norton, Andrew and Beni Cakitaki, *Mapping Australian
    Higher Education 2016*, Grattan Institute, Carlton, 2016.

Norton, Andrew, Julie Sonnemann and Cassie McGannon, *The
    Online Evolution: When Technology Meets Tradition in
    Higher Education*, Grattan Institute, Carlton, 2013.

O'Farrell, Patrick, *UNSW, a Portrait: The University of New
    South Wales 1949–1999*, UNSW Press, Sydney, 1999.

O'Keefe, Brendan, 'UNSW Singapore Campus Doomed to Fail',
    The Australian, 27 June 2007. http://www.theaustralian.
    com.au/higher-education/unsw-singapore-campus-doomed-
    to-fail/news-story/f5e86304426b1b57df267345157a4397
    (viewed May 2017).

Page, Scott E, 'Path Dependence', *Quarterly Journal of Political
    Science*, vol. 1, 2006, pp. 87–115.

Pelikan, Jaroslav, *The Idea of the University—A Re-examination*, Yale University Press, New Haven, CT, 1992.

Perry, Paul Francis, *The Rise and Fall of Practically Everybody: An Account of Student Political Activity at Monash University, 1965–1972*, self-published, Balaclava, 1973.

Persse, Michael, 'Wentworth, William Charles (1790–1872)', *Australian Dictionary of Biography*, vol. 2, Melbourne University Publishing, Carlton, 1967. http://adb.anu.edu. au/biography/wentworth-william-charles-2782 (viewed May 2017).

Pierson, Paul, 'The New Politics of the Welfare State', *World Politics*, vol. 48, no. 2, 1996, pp. 143–79.

—— *Politics in Time: History, Institutions, and Social Analysis*, Princeton University Press, Princeton, NJ, 2004.

Pietsch, Tamson, *Empire of Scholars: Universities, Networks and the British Academic World, 1850–1939*, Manchester University Press, Manchester, 2013.

Queensland, Legislative Assembly, *Parliamentary Debates*, 3 November 1959, pp. 1088–9.

Quirke, Noel, *Preparing for the Future: A History of Griffith University 1971–1996*, Boolarong Press, Brisbane, 1996.

Rayson, Hannie, *Life after George*, Currency Press, Strawberry Hills, 2000.

Report of the Committee on Australian Universities (The Murray Report), Commonwealth of Australia, Canberra, 1957.

Rosen, Andrew S, *Change.edu: Rebooting for the New Talent Economy*, Kaplan Publishing, New York, 2011.

Schumpeter, Joseph A, *Capitalism, Socialism and Democracy*, Unwin University Books, London, 1974 (f.p. 1942).

—— *The Economics and Sociology of Capitalism*, edited by Richard Swedberg, Princeton University Press, Princeton, NJ, 1991.

Schwartz, Herman, 'Down the Wrong Path: Path Dependence, Increasing Returns, and Historical Institutionalism', Department of Politics, University of Virginia, Charlottesville, VA, 2004. http://www.people.virginia. edu/~hms2f/Path.pdf (viewed August 2017).

Selleck, Richard JW, *The Shop: The University of Melbourne, 1850–1939*, Melbourne University Press, Carlton, 2003.

Serle, Geoffrey, *John Monash: A Biography*, Melbourne University Publishing, Carlton, 1982.

Smithipedia, 'President Jill Ker Conway', 2017. https://sophia.smith.edu/blog/smithipedia/administration/president-jill-ker-conway/ (viewed May 2017).

Stinchcombe, Arthur, *Constructing Social Theories*, Harcourt Brace, New York, 1968.

Stoppard, Tom, *The Invention of Love*, Faber, London, 1998.

Strachey, Lytton, *Eminent Victorians*, Garden City, New York, 1918.

Thomas, Inigo, 'The Chase', *London Review of Books*, vol. 38, no. 20, 20 October 2016, pp. 15–18.

Thomis, Malcolm I, *A Place of Light & Learning: The University of Queensland's First Seventy-five Years*, University of Queensland Press, St Lucia, 1985.

Thrift, Nigel, 'The University of Life', *New Literary History*, vol. 47, nos 2–3, 2016, pp. 399–417.

Toren, Matthew, 'Top 100 Entrepreneurs Who Made Millions without a College Degree', *Business Insider Australia*, 20 January 2011. http://www.businessinsider.com.au/top-100-entrepreneurs-who-made-millions-without-a-college-degree-2011-1?r=US&IR=T (viewed May 2017).

Trow, Martin, 'Elite and Mass Higher Education: American Models and European Realities', in Swedish National Board of Universities and Colleges (ed.), *Research into Higher Education: Processes and Structures. Information on Higher Education in Sweden*, Conference proceedings, Stockholm, 1979.

Trowbridge, Cassidy, 'University of Phoenix Parent Accepts Federal Amendments for Buyout Approval', *Phoenix Business Journal*, 21 December 2016. http://www.bizjournals.com/phoenix/news/2016/12/21/university-of-phoenix-parent-accepts-federal.html (viewed May 2017).

Turney, Clifford, Ursula Bygott and Peter Chippendale, *Australia's First: A History of the University of Sydney, Vol. 1: 1850–1939*, Hale & Iremonger, Sydney, 1991.

Udacity, 'About Us', 2017. https://www.udacity.com/us (viewed May 2017).

Universities Australia, *Offshore Programs of Australian Universities*, Canberra, April 2014.

—— *Higher Education and Research Facts and Figures: November 2015*, Canberra, 2015.

University of New South Wales, *History*, 2017. http:// www.unsw.edu.au/about-us/university/history (viewed May 2017).

University of New South Wales—University Archives, *Broken Hill Division of the University of New South Wales*, 2014. https://www.recordkeeping.unsw.edu.au/documents/A679-BrokenHill.pdf (viewed May 2017).

University of Sydney Act 1850, United Kingdom. http:// www.foundingdocs.gov.au/resources/transcripts/nsw10_doc_1850.pdf (viewed May 2017).

University of Western Australia, 'How Many Students Does It Take to Dig a Hole?', *Stories from the Archives*, 2015. ttp://www.web.uwa.edu.au/university/history/centenary/archive-stories/reflection-pond (viewed June 2017).

van Vught, Frans, 'Mission Diversity and Reputation in Higher Education', *Higher Education Policy*, vol. 21, 2008, pp. 151–74.

Victoria, Legislative Assembly, *Parliamentary Debates*, 1 April 1958, p. 3935.

Wackett, Murray, 'Theme and Variations—Music at Murdoch', in Murdoch University (ed.), *Murdoch Voices: The First 40 Years at Murdoch University*, Murdoch University, Perth, 2015, pp. 122–27.

Walsh, Jill Paton, *Lapsing*, Black Swan, London, 1986.

Watson, Don, 'Goodness and Wisdom in Bundoora', in La Trobe University (ed.), 2017, *From the Paddock to the Agora: Fifty Years of La Trobe University*, La Trobe University Press in conjunction with Black Inc., Carlton, 2017, pp. 11–30.

Whitehead, Alfred N, *Science and the Modern World*, Pelican, London, 1938 (f.p. 1925).

Wildavsky, Ben, *The Great Brain Race: How Global Universities Are Reshaping the World*, Princeton University Press, Princeton, NJ, 2010.

Williams, Bruce, *Liberal Education and Useful Knowledge: A Brief History of the University of Sydney 1850–2000*, Chancellor's Committee, University of Sydney, Sydney, 2002.

Wilson, Woodrow, 'Princeton in the Nation's Service', Address
    delivered to the Princeton University sesquicentennial
    celebration, 21 October 1896. http://infoshare1.princeton.
    edu/libraries/firestone/rbsc/mudd/online_ex/wilsonline/
    indn8nsvc.html (viewed June 2017).
Wolf, Alison, 'Degrees of Failure: Why It's Time to Reconsider
    How We Run Our Universities', *Prospect*, 14 July 2017.
    https://www.prospectmagazine.co.uk/magazine/degrees-
    of-failure-do-universities-actually-do-any-good (viewed
    August 2017).
Wood, Graeme, 'The Future of College?', *The Atlantic*,
    September 2014. https://www.theatlantic.com/magazine/
    archive/2014/09/the-future-of-college/375071/ (viewed
    May 2017).
Woolley, Liz, 'How the Railway Changed Oxford', *Oxfordshire
    Local History Association Journal*, vol. 9, no. 4, 2013–14,
    pp. 18–43. http://www.olha.org.uk/wp-admin/images/
    OLHAvol9no4pp18-43Woolley.compressed.pdf (viewed
    May 2017).
—— 'The Coming of the Railway to Oxford', *South Oxford
    Community Centre*, 2016. http://www.southoxford.
    org/local-history-in-south-oxford/interesting-aspects-of-
    grandpont-and-south-oxford-s-history/the-coming-of-the-
    railway-to-oxford (viewed May 2017).

INDEX